BIG *Thrift* energy

Published by Blue Star Press

PO Box 5622, Bend, OR 97708

contact@bluestarpress.com | www.bluestarpress.com

Cover and Interior Design by Megan Kesting

Photography by Agnes Lopez

ISBN 9781950968619

Printed in Colombia

10 9 8 7 6 5 4 3 2 1

For Joy. Forever.

Big Thrift Energy

The Art and Thrill of Finding Vintage Treasures—
Plus Tips for Making Old Feel New

Virginia Chamlee

BLUE·STAR
PRESS

Contents

Introduction

DO YOU REMEMBER YOUR FIRST CRUSH? Not the one from your preschool days that only lasted for an hour or so. I'm talking knockdown, drag-out, can't-stop-thinking-about-them infatuation. The kind that keeps you up at night, quickens your heartbeat, and consumes your thoughts for minutes, hours, even days.

That's what a great thrift find is like for me.

The night before I visit a new thrift store, go on an all-day flea market trip, or attend an early-morning estate sale can only be described with one word: butterflies.

Scouring vintage shops and thrift stores for beautiful, unique pieces is my favorite thing to do. Over the years, I've found pieces that are not just one of a kind but also incredibly valuable: a $20,000 Goyard trunk for $90; an $800 Christian Dior tweed cape for $10; and even a signed work of art by an artist in the Smithsonian's permanent collection, found for pennies at a Habitat for Humanity resale shop.

The biggest thrill of vintage shopping is that it's a never-ending quest. Even if you find a 1950s Lanvin dress for $2 at an estate sale, you could still pop into a thrift store 5 minutes later and find something even better (as was the case with the afore-mentioned Goyard trunk). You never know what you're about to find. Just like the early days of any good crush, it's all about the chase.

Of course, sometimes crushes are unrequited. I have my bad days with vintage shopping, when I drive 3 hours to go to more than a dozen shops and leave every single one empty handed.

But you know what? I always pick myself up and do it all over again, because that's what infatuation is all about. And this particular love affair started early for me.

MY THRIFTING JOURNEY

My grandmother raised me in northeast Florida, which, idyllic as it may be in natural beauty, is not exactly known for its designer wares. Ever the entrepreneur, she seized on the then-burgeoning Shabby Chic design trend. (This was the '90s, folks.) She launched a business from our home, buying containers of carefully distressed furniture and reselling them at sales that she hosted monthly in our living room and front yard. One step into her makeshift storefront and customers were greeted with oversize chippy armoires; rustic, cream-colored cabinets; and queen-size wooden beds begging for a pink-and-white duvet.

To supplement her inventory, she dragged me to estate sales, live auctions, and thrift stores, looking for pieces that would fit right into her well-heeled customers' homes: botanical prints in bamboo frames, sculptural objects to add style to a bookshelf, and stacks of books in complementary hues.

I slowly got hooked on the adrenaline rush of placing the winning bid in a live auction or unearthing a mint-condition work of art that was the perfect aesthetic match for a console table in an upcoming shipment. My grandmother's business quickly outgrew our living room, so she and her business partner transitioned to a brick-and-mortar space: a large booth in an antiques gallery.

I visited Beaches Antique Gallery every day after dance class and nearly every weekend. I did my homework while perched on a velvet Milo Baughman chair in a neighboring booth and passed the time by roaming the aisles, memorizing the signatures on canvases and labels on sofa cushions.

My days spent at the gallery soon began to intersect with another passion I'd picked up very early on: fashion. Prior to launching her furniture business, my grandmother had owned a women's clothing boutique in northeast Georgia, selling new pieces from labels such as Diane von Furstenberg and Liz Claiborne—and even tailoring the clothes herself.

My grandmother's love for the craftsmanship and history of clothes rubbed off on me. By the time I was 12, I had a subscription to *InStyle*. I would read the magazine from cover to cover, running my fingers over the photos in hopes of absorbing the style of the models donning labels like Donna Karan and Emanuel Ungaro.

While my preteen dreams skewed champagne, my budget was decidedly more cherry cola. Fortunately, through the wonders of picking and vintage shopping—and the wealth of information I had gleaned from magazines and my grandmother—I was able to amass a pretty noteworthy collection of designer goods without breaking my childhood piggy bank.

Estate sales,
live auctions,
and thrift stores —
oh my

Shop what
feels *authentic*
to you

I remember my first Mid-Century painting: an oversize oil on canvas of a horse in moody dark blues that I hung on my bedroom wall. Then there's one of my still-to-this-day favorite pieces of jewelry: a 1980s gold bangle, printed with the word "Lagerfeld," each letter of the iconic designer's name capitalized and spelled out in a different color. An identical bangle—now a piece of fashion history—recently sold on 1stDibs for roughly $1,200. I found mine at an antiques fair in 2005 for $15.

I never stopped buying vintage, and in 2015, I decided to get more serious about selling it. I created an online store, narrowing down my buys and focusing on an aesthetic that was the most "me": colorful, sculptural, unique, and well made. Within a couple of years, my side business had taken off, evolving into a hobby that at times generated more profit than my full-time job as a writer and reporter.

I am by no means an expert on antiques and have certainly made my fair share of mistakes when it comes to buying and selling vintage. But over the years, I have amassed a lot of knowledge about how to navigate the (admittedly intimidating and not always inclusive) world of antiques, and find the good stuff. With this book, my goal is to share a little bit of what I've learned in hopes that you will also fall for the thrill of thrifting—and to make things easier for you along the way.

I've included lots of tips that have helped me over the years, stories of my own favorite finds, and photos of how I've curated these goods in my own home. Because as much as I love admiring the perfect curation of a room styled by a top interior designer, I also believe it's important for homes to be personal and approachable rather than perfect. We do live in them, after all. While I might adhere to a few tried-and-true design rules, I am a big believer in experimentation: checkerboard can be a neutral, and mixing patterns can warm up a space. My style is not for everyone, and yours shouldn't be either! So take inspiration where you can and leave the rest. And always, always shop and style in a way that feels authentic to you.

At thrift stores and antiques malls, you're bound to find something for every aesthetic, from Postmodern abstract art straight out of the pages of *Architectural Digest* to minimalist Danish designs just begging to be taken home and Instagrammed. Love the street style of 1980s New York? You can find vintage Adidas windbreakers and designer bags if you visit Goodwill often enough. Is a more traditional aesthetic more your speed? Estate sales are full of all the dog and pony prints, upholstered settees, and toile lampshades your preppy heart desires.

And yes, my heart still does beat for all those things and more: all the brass lamps, the punchy patterned pillows, the silk blouses, the wrap dresses, the high-waisted trousers, and everything in between. All these years later, I'm not tired of vintage shopping. I still get butterflies.

HOW TO USE THIS BOOK

Good design never goes out of style, and even the most well-known interior designers turn to the past when outfitting their clients' homes. It's easy to head to a big-box store and snag a factory-made dresser for a couple hundred bucks, but you can find more unique, well-made, and affordable pieces in vintage and thrift shops. Incidentally, buying vintage is also a stylish way to be kinder to the planet: Antiques last longer, and buying used items keeps them out of landfills. Who can argue with the feel-good factor of that?

But shopping for vintage can be intimidating. How do you know if a piece is worth the price? How do you separate the good stuff from the junk? How do you navigate the piles of merchandise in a thrift store? With *Big Thrift Energy*, I've aimed to answer those questions and more, using the flow of the book to mirror the cadence of my own journey, from research and buying to cleaning and styling—and yes, even selling.

The first two sections of the book are all about shopping and everything that comes before: how to create an inspiration board, some 101-level vintage design, and how to best traverse the vast shopping landscape, whether in person or online (hello-o-o-o, Facebook Marketplace). I've included tried-and-true tips for negotiating prices (which you'll want to do at a flea market), as well as some insider knowledge on which parts of the country are often stocked with which type of stuff (think: Mid-Century Mod in all the Detroit suburbs).

The next section focuses on styling, because sometimes the hard part isn't finding a diamond in the rough but knowing what to do with it! Here, you'll find a few DIY ideas for upcycling something old into something "you," as well as styling tips that go beyond color palettes and fabric pairings (like how to use a bench as a coffee table, or ways to get that "effortless" layered look).

The last portion of the book offers advice on selling vintage, whether you're looking to off-load a few items or start your side hustle. Not to sound like I'm trying to get you involved in a patterned-leggings pyramid scheme, but the biggest benefit of an entrepreneurial venture is the possibility of unlimited earnings potential—and you won't even have to recruit 20 other people to do it! If you find yourself addicted to the rush of unearthing treasures and filled with a passion for beautiful things, you can make good money flipping vintage. But you'll need to put in some serious work.

Shopping for vintage is fun, but it can be overwhelming if you aren't used to waking up at 3 a.m. for an estate sale (been there), making a low offer on a Mid-Century dresser on Craigslist (done that), or learning which times of year are the best for visiting flea markets (bought the T-shirt). With *Big Thrift Energy*, think of me as your guide, sharing tips and insights gleaned from years spent treasure hunting and making the old look new. We're in this together. Now let's go shopping, shall we?

PART ONE

KNOW BEFORE YOU GO

THE THOUGHT OF GOING "ANTIQUING" MIGHT CONJURE up a specific image if you're a rookie: stacks of well-worn vintage magazines sitting atop a perfectly distressed French provincial table; a leather armchair with gleaming chrome legs, flanked by a Lucite stool and curved wooden floor lamp. Everything perfectly merchandised, priced to sell, and already styled to perfection.

The reality is much different.

On any given day you find me at the thrift store, I'm probably on the floor looking for the maker's mark beneath a dining table, or pulling two dozen tourist-themed shot glasses off a shelf in an effort to get a closer look at a vase stuffed in a corner.

For every antiques mall full of styled booths, there are dozens of thrift and charity shops that are packed to the brim with bad dorm room posters and "No talkie before coffee" mugs. Even the shops with all the novelty mugs have treasure, I promise; it just takes a bit of practice to find it.

If you're new to the world of vintage, one foot inside a huge antiques mall or thrift store—and one look at the gobs and gobs of trinkets therein—might overwhelm you and fill you with a sense of dread.

I get it. I've taken dozens of friends out "Goodwill hunting" with me, only to have them sigh in frustration and declare the day a loss before we've made it past aisle one in the first store.

There's an art and a science to hunting for vintage treasures, and once you master it, that overwhelming feeling will be replaced with the thrill and adrenaline I experience every time I go out on a quest.

That being said, you would never run a marathon without training first, right? Similarly, you'll want to do a little bit of preparation before heading out into the big, wide world of vintage. Trust me, it will make the experience feel much more manageable.

Define Your Style

RUNNING INTO THE FIRST GOODWILL YOU SEE without having an idea of your personal style is not a good idea. It's kind of like joining a dating app without having an idea of what you're looking for: You run the risk on swiping right on everything in sight.

It's really easy to get carried away when antiquing; without much sticker shock to worry about, you might be tempted to load up the cart with anything even remotely cute. But we don't want to do that for the sake of a) the environment (thrifting is sustainable, but not if you start buying so much that most of it winds up in a landfill anyway) and b) your sanity (i.e., the potential to be cast on an episode of *Hoarders*).

There's also the flip side, which is the challenge of being drawn to something interesting but lacking the confidence or style savvy to know what to do with it. As a result, you become too shy to buy anything. Defining your own style will help you avoid both of these pitfalls.

Defining a "look" or aesthetic you want can help you stay focused, reduce feelings of being overwhelmed, and allow you to be more strategic so you'll have better results in the long run. Whatever your eye is drawn to—bright colors, clean lines, sexy shapes—let that drive your overall aesthetic.

ORGANIC
SHAPES

ICONIC
MID-CENTURY
DESIGN

PAIRS **AND**
SYMMETRY

CLEAN
LINES

PUNCHY
COLORS AND
PATTERNS

CLASSIC
WELL-MADE
FURNITURE

RATTAN
AND
WICKER

ABSTRACT
MINIMALLY-HUED
ARTWORK

MARBLE

THE OCCASIONAL PIECE
OF **PALM BEACH-STYLE**
RATTAN, BUT ALSO A
NEOCLASSICAL BUST
(AND ALSO ABSTRACT
ART! AND ALSO THAT
VERY TRADITIONAL 1800S
PORTRAIT IS COOL,
TOO! **AND ALSO** ...)

POPS OF **GREEN**
ONLY **PLANTS** CAN PROVIDE

TEXTILES

TRADITIONAL

When shopping, you'll want
to keep an eye out for the
classics: chinoiserie ginger
jars, architectural art, and
well-made pieces of furniture
that can be easily reupholstered to suit your taste.

COLLECTOR

If you have a penchant for
selecting "All of the above" on a
quiz, you probably have a taste for
variety. In that case, keep your eyes
peeled for anything interesting and
well made that you can layer to
your heart's content: vintage
National Geographic magazines,
antique busts of all shapes and
sizes, stone or marble boxes to
store all your knickknacks—you
get the idea.

BOHEMIAN

Look for all things rattan—plus
terra-cotta planters, oversize shag rugs,
and plenty of patterns.

MODERN MINIMALIST

Be on the hunt for specific
materials: chrome, light-toned
woods, marble, as well as
minimalist art and sculpture
(plus maybe some black-and-
white photography scored at
an estate sale).

My office is like the island of misfit finds, home to everything from a vintage death mask (yup, it's exactly what you think it is) to my beloved (and very cheeky) word art—both estate sale finds

ASS
EMB
LER

ASS
UMA
BLE

ASS
URA
NCE

ASS
AIL
ANT

ASS
ASS
INS

ASS
ORT
ING

ASS
ERT
ION

ASS
OCI
ATE

ASS
IDU
OUS

POTION

Do Your Online Research

AS KIM ZOLCIAK-BIERMANN, OF THE REAL HOUSEWIVES OF ATLANTA fame, eloquently once sang, "Research me, you'll find me. Click them keys and Google me."

Clearly, she was embodying a thrifted Vladimir Kagan couch when she penned those lyrics.

The internet has opened a world of opportunity for vintage hounds, making it easier than ever to research artists, furniture makers, and brand names—information that used to be much more exclusive and harder to track down. No longer does one have to spend hours attempting to make out the signature on a painting or sifting through old design books to try to identify the provenance of a piece of furniture.

Research is a crucial and, frankly, really fun aspect of shopping vintage. Continually broadening your knowledge of vintage makers and design styles means that over time, you will be able to spot something amazing, even if it's hidden behind a bunch of junk.

Thrift stores are often a jumbled mess of merchandise, and antiques stores aren't always much better. It's difficult for your eye to even know where to land when you're looking at a wall with approximately 10,000 paintings hung on it. By laying a solid foundation, you'll be much more likely to discover those rare, unique, and even valuable pieces that will add interest to your home.

While there are several great websites that can help you determine the maker or value of a piece (more on that on page 23), there are some sites I recommend perusing before you even start to shop. They will help you stay current on what's trending in the world of design, what sells if you're looking to turn a profit, and what to look for when you go shopping.

SITES I LOVE

Chairish and 1stDibs are excellent places to research art, furniture, and even fashion. If I find a piece and don't know who the maker is, those are my go-to resources. (Just plug some keywords into the search tab and look through the results until you find something similar.)

Other great resources include auction houses and vintage forums. Sites such as Artprice, Invaluable, and LiveAuctioneers allow registered users to research and compare prices of items sold at auction. Found a corset but can't determine how old it is? One of the users at the online forum Vintage Fashion Guild can probably help. Picked up a 1980s abstract piece but can't read the label on the back? Head to Collectors Weekly, where vintage fiends often upload photos of their latest thrift finds to determine the story behind them.

If all else fails, turn to social media. I've had luck in the past by uploading a pic of a find on Instagram and asking, "Does anyone know who made this?"

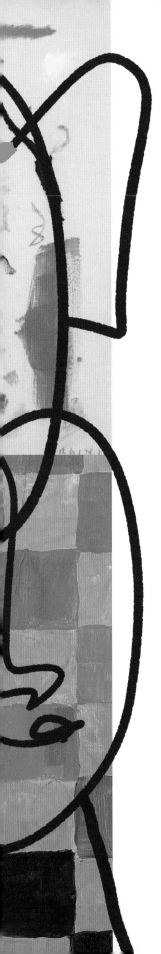

1STDIBS | *1stdibs.com* | Luxury online retailer specializing in ultra-high-end items from interior design to fine art and jewelry. Excellent resource to determine how much a thrifted or estate treasure might actually be worth (or, at least, how high-end vintage dealers are marking it)

ARTISTS' SIGNATURES | *artistssignatures.com* | Literally a website full of photos of artists' signatures, categorized alphabetically so you can compare the signature on that 1960s landscape to determine if it's made by someone "important"

CHAIRISH | *chairish.com* | Online luxury retailer specializing in well-made, glamorous, and often trendy vintage art and furnishings. Great resource to determine the maker of an item and get an idea of what's trending in the world of design. Serves as both an inspiration for how to decorate your own home and a way to search for who made an item you find in the wild

COLLECTORS WEEKLY | *collectorsweekly.com* | Veritable buffet of blog posts and articles about rare and antique items, from toys to jewelry. "Show & Tell" feature is especially fun; serves as a forum where collectors can showcase their finds

LIVEAUCTIONEERS | *liveauctioneers.com* | Massive online marketplace for art, antiques, and collectibles. Best part is auction price results database, which allows you to search historical hammer prices (an inside term for "winning bids") dating back to 1999, so you can see how much items have sold for in the past and get a sense of their value

VINTAGE FASHION GUILD | *vintagefashionguild.org* | An organization dedicated to the promotion and preservation of vintage fashion. Founded by vintage sellers. Contains a wealth of information about fashion, including tips on care and cleaning, plus identification guides on everything from fabric to labels

WORTHPOINT | *worthpoint.com* | Subscription-based database that houses thousands of maker's marks and artists' signatures. Can tell you more about what your item is made of (if you're able to narrow down to the appropriate brands), where and when it was made, and the specific brand

MID-CENTURY MODERN

ARTS & CRAFT

HOLLYWOOD REGENCY

POSTMODERN

POSTMODERN

HOLLYWOOD REGENCY

MID-CENTURY MODERN

Design Styles through the Eras

SUCCESSFULLY SHOPPING FOR ANTIQUES IS ALL about having the confidence to recognize something is special—without being so cocky that you snag a $5 paper IKEA lamp you could have sworn was a Noguchi valued at $800.

But even if you don't know who Noguchi is (I promise, you don't have to), you should at least be able to discern design and whether something is well made before you begin to dig. A broad knowledge base will come in handy, helping you build confidence before you even begin to fill your shopping cart. Here are the basics.

ARTS & CRAFTS

Era: 1860s–1920s
Description: American, craftsman-made furnishings known for a reliance on high-quality woods, such as cherry and quartersawn white oak, and a medieval influence. Tramp art—in which accessories like frames and boxes are made from discarded materials, such as scraps of wood or cigar boxes—generally falls under this category.
Designers and labels to look for: Charles Rohlfs, Harvey Ellis, Stickley

ART DECO

Era: 1920s–1930s
Description: Short for Arts Décoratifs; characterized by metal, rich accents and colors, geometry, and decadent details
Designers and labels to look for: Paul Follot, Émile-Jacques Ruhlmann, Eileen Gray

MID-CENTURY MODERN

Era: 1940s–1960s
Description: Post–World War II movement rooted in clean lines, organic shapes, simplicity, and functionality
Designers and labels to look for: Herman Miller, Knoll, Eames, Eero Saarinen, Harry Bertoia

POSTMODERN

Era: 1970s–1990s
Description: Noted for its use of bold primary colors (and later, muted and even retro tones), clean-lined and asymmetric shapes, and pop culture references (think: the flashier moments of the 1980s)
Designers and labels to look for: Memphis Group/Ettore Sottsass, Michael Graves, Judy Kensley McKie

HOLLYWOOD REGENCY

Era: Inspired by the 1920s–1950s but often made in the 1960s–1970s
Description: Opulence, glitz, and glam reign supreme, with designs characterized by sumptuous materials (fur, velvet) and gleaming accents (brass, chrome, anything that seems like it came from Palm Beach)
Designers and labels to look for: Charles Hollis Jones, Dorothy Draper, William Haines, Karl Springer

Build *confidence* before you fill your shopping cart

MAYBE THIS IS HOW IT STARTS

TOO MUCH

Be Prepared

IF YOU'RE JUST DIPPING A TOE INTO the wide waters of vintage, the sheer number of options might leave your head spinning. Here are a few tips to help make the process a lot less overwhelming.

KNOW WHAT YOU NEED

As with grocery shopping, you'll first want to prioritize the things you need.

For instance, if you're in desperate need of a dresser, go out and look specifically for dressers. Just don't limit yourself to one single color, shape, or era. You may have a style in mind but fall in love with one that's completely different and perfect for your space. This is what makes vintage hunting so much more exciting than ordering from IKEA.

Just don't get too desperate if you can avoid it. If you're hosting a dinner party and in need of some new glasses and flatware, take time to pop into several shops to do some comparison shopping. Don't settle! Go to at least a half dozen shops to find something that really resonates with you. (And don't be afraid to mix and match: Pairing a funky '80s platter with a more traditional blue-and-white set of china could be really fun.)

HAVE AN IDEA OF WHAT YOU WANT

Even on the days when I don't need something specific, I still have an idea of what I want. I keep an ongoing list of "dream items," which helps keep me focused when I'm out in the wild.

You can start collecting images of items you like—maybe it's the shape of a vase or the colors in a particular painting—by saving them on Pinterest or Instagram. When you are out shopping, you can refer back to this digital vision board so if you see something in a similar colorway, pattern, or shape, you'll know you need to snag it. (Bonus: You'll already have a reference image of how to style it, too.) Getting into this habit will help guide your eye to the items that resonate most with you.

REMAIN OPEN TO SURPRISES

Sticking with the grocery store analogy, you'll also want to leave some room for surprise treats and irresistible deals.

Thrift stores, estate sales, and antiques shops are home to so many "never seen anything quite like this before" items, so always keep an open mind—while also being careful not to hoard or buy anything you're not confident you can use. Part of being open is being willing to see an item not for what it is, but what it could be. For instance, you might not have room in your cupboard for that funky collection of Italian plates you found at the Salvation Army, but maybe you have an empty wall where they could hang. Case in point: For months, I would buy vintage tablecloths and quilts without having anywhere to put them, simply because I fell in love with the patterns. Months later, when I was looking for a new console table, I had a light bulb moment and threw one of the quilts over my old console. I had a newish table and made use of my old quilt to boot.

STICK TO WHAT SPEAKS TO YOU

Want a surefire hack to make the process of vintage shopping much more manageable? Only buy what truly speaks to you, even if it isn't some high-value item you'll pass on to your kids one day. Some of my favorite pieces are those that I knew I wouldn't be able to get out of my head had I left them behind. It's more important that a piece be unique than created by a well-known brand.

CHECKITY CHECK- LIST

THINGS TO HAVE ON YOUR PERSON AT ALL TIMES WHEN VINTAGE SHOPPING:

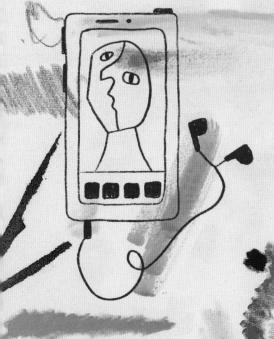

→ TAPE MEASURE

→ SOLD TAGS: Some estate sales will require you to bring your own for larger items. Be sure to include your name and phone number on the tag.

→ SMARTPHONE: You'll want to be able to Google an artist's signature or label on a piece of furniture to determine if it's a valuable piece.

→ CASH: Most yard sales and garage sales—and some thrift stores—still only accept cash.

→ BLANKETS OR TOWELS: These come in handy when wrapping glass items or keeping things from moving around in your car.

→ MAGNET: This is super helpful if you're into buying brass, copper, or aluminum pieces—a magnet won't stick to those, so if you can adhere a magnet to something that looks brass, it's probably metal with brass-colored plating.

Know Where to Shop

ONE OF THE REASONS ANTIQUING IS SO INTIMIDATING is due to the sheer variety of shopping experiences. There are antiques malls, which are full of booths styled by different dealers. There are estate sales, which can be really upscale and well organized or a jumbled mess offering half-used boxes of aluminum foil. And there are thrift stores (my personal fave), which have tons of inventory, generally low prices, and special sale days, but they require a lot of patience and tenacity. Some venues are better for certain things (for example, estate sales are great for furniture, as it's generally very well kept) and some require way more time than others (where you at, flea markets?). In an attempt to ease you into the process, I've broken each venue down into levels, ranked from beginner to advanced, and outlined the amount of time you're likely to spend at each.

THE ANTIQUES MALL

Level: Beginner
Minimum time requirement: 1–2 hours
Negotiation expected? Yes

There are antiques shops—the mom-and-pop brick-and-mortars that have trinkets, furniture, and other odds and ends from various eras—and then there are antiques malls. Like any other shopping mall, an antiques mall is home to vendors, each showcasing its wares in a booth or stall. The dealers themselves don't necessarily staff the place, but management and staffers are almost always happy to call dealers to see if they'll go lower on particular items.

Negotiating is expected. You can expect to get a discount of 10 to 15 percent (maybe even more if it's a piece that you've noticed has been on display for several months). Some dealers won't negotiate at all, but others might surprise you.

TIP! Many antique malls will upload photos of new merchandise to Instagram or Facebook, so be sure to hit that "Follow" button. Search for individual dealers as well as the mall itself. Sometimes both will have a social media presence, which will give you a great head start.

FLEA MARKETS

Level: Beginner/intermediate
Minimum time requirement: 4–8 hours
Negotiation expected? Yes

Flea markets are like thrifting on steroids. These tend to be weekly or monthly full-day (or weekend) events. You can spend hours picking, haggling, and buying, with the added excitement of having an excuse to eat corn dogs and other food cooked on a stick.

Keep in mind that there are different levels of flea markets. There are true flea markets, where items are dirt cheap, and then there are high-end experiences masquerading as flea markets, which are more curated and costly. Each has its own appeal.

For true deals, you'll want to hit up the lesser-known, less-expensive markets. If you want to be dazzled, check out the massive, gorgeous, over-the-top events, such as Brimfield and Round Top or the slightly smaller–but-no-less-amazing markets, such as Renninger's, in Florida and Pennsylvania. The deals you can find at flea markets will vary month to month, so keep the time of year in mind. (For instance, a dealer once told me that in Florida, most of the snowbirds come to flea markets in winter, so dealers mark up their prices in January and February.)

TIP! As with an estate sale, prices tend to get lowered on the final day, since dealers want to off-load their merchandise. The only problem with waiting until the final day is, of course, that the market will be picked over by then. But you can find some excellent deals this way if you're lucky!

EXTRA TIP! This is the dorkiest thing I will ever implore you to do, but bringing a collapsible cart with wheels to a flea market is truly the best idea ever. It allows you to have free hands for browsing and to carry more stuff. Don't forget bubble wrap or newspaper to wrap fragile and smaller items, so they don't bump around and break in your supercool cart.

Flea markets are thrifting on *steroids*

ONLINE MARKETPLACES

Level: Intermediate
Minimum time requirement: 1 hour
Negotiation expected? Yes (that's kind of the entire premise of OfferUp)

Craigslist, Facebook Marketplace, and OfferUp can be gold mines for deals, but don't assume that just because these markets are online, they're easy. I find online marketplaces to be even more difficult to navigate than a thrift store!

There are people who will tell you that the best way to shop online marketplaces is to narrow your search and be as specific as possible. Those people are wrong. I like to take the opposite approach, going broad and seeing what crops up.

Here's why: If you type the words "Vladimir Kagan sofa" into the Craigslist search bar, you may very well see a couple of results that are just what you're looking for. But the people selling them know exactly what they have and—more often than not—the price will reflect that.

What you really want to find are wares being sold by people who might not know the worth of the item. Maybe they're getting rid of something they inherited, off-loading a thrift-store find they never bothered to research, or just want the item gone ASAP. And the only way to find these gems is to do a generic search and sift through all the results.

This can be painstaking, eye-watering work, because most of these sellers write vague titles and descriptions on their listings.

For instance, on Facebook Marketplace I once found a pair of stunning 1980s side tables by Philippines-based designer Betty Cobonpue for $30 (which, for reference, are very rare and retail for upwards of $1,200). They were listed as "wicker tables" (never mind that the tables aren't even made of wicker)!

Searching generic terms (lamp, table, wicker table) and spending hours scrolling through results can be absolutely mind numbing, but the payoff is worth it. I once found a drop-dead gorgeous 1980s glass-topped dining table with a hand-carved wooden base in the shape of oversize swans. It was listed on Facebook Marketplace as "table," with no mention of the swans, which are kind of the whole point.

TIP! If you're in the market for something from a specific era, check online market-places every day. Consistency will reward you. (Plus, the algorithms are pretty spot on, so over time, the sites will start showing you listings they think you'd like—e.g., Mid-Century furniture—without having to search.)

THRIFT STORES

Level: Intermediate/advanced

Minimum time requirement: 1–8 hours

Negotiation expected? No (Items are generally priced as marked, and the funds are almost always going to a charity)

Goodwill, the Salvation Army, your local secondhand shop—thrift stores are my favorite places to hunt for vintage. They may sound basic, but for the uninitiated, they can be daunting and difficult to shop, given their sheer size, volume, and impressive commitment to disorganization. Here are a few tips for what to do when you're looking to snag something that's worth all the inevitable digging.

Look everywhere: Yes, you'll want to check all the obvious spots in a thrift store—the clothing racks, the home decor section—but you'll also need to look closer, because many items can get hidden. I've seen thrift stores that display art and mirrors against the wall behind racks of clothing or hang paintings in a hallway leading to a bathroom (or even in the bathroom itself).

Examine items closely: There are a few surefire ways to identify an item's provenance. If it's a chair, you'll want to pick up the cushions to see if there's a label underneath. If it's a painting, check the lower corners, the upper corners, and the back of the canvas for markings or signatures. If it's a coat, look for tags near the interior pockets, not just the back of the neck.

Do a quality check: Even if there are no tags signifying the designer of an item, you can check for quality, at the very least. What's the item made of? If it's a blouse made of wool, cashmere, or silk, it will likely hold up well and keep its shape. The same goes for furniture made of heavy woods, marbles, stones, or metals like brass. If it will still look great in 10 years, regardless of whether it has a designer label on it, buy it. Keep in mind, though, that even the nicest materials can be damaged, so be sure to examine items closely to ensure they aren't beyond repair. (Chipped glass, ripped leather, and snagged wool are all no-gos in my book.)

Find a honeypot: I am an advocate of shopping as many thrift stores as you can, as often as you can, but I also believe in finding that one honeypot that you seem to be able to draw from again and again.

In northeast Florida, there's an interior designer–owned, high-end shop that I discovered unloads its unsold merchandise to a nearby thrift store. How did I discover this hidden gem? I happened to be shopping one day and noticed that

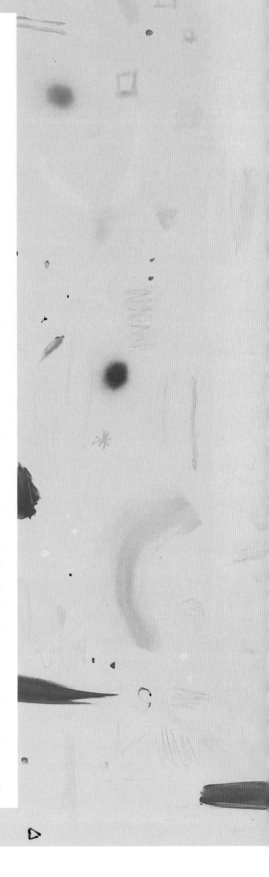

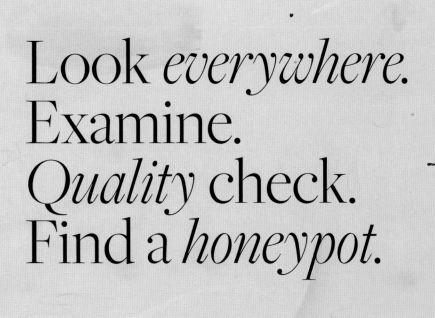

Look *everywhere.*
Examine.
Quality check.
Find a *honeypot.*

at least 10 items I found all had the original price tags on them. The staff at the thrift store told me that they get deliveries of unsold furniture, art, and accessories from this particular boutique at least once a month. Needless to say, it became a biweekly stop for me. If you happen to notice that the thrift store price tag is covering a much heftier price tag from a local boutique, you might want to visit that thrift shop once a week to see if they continue getting in the local goods.

TIP! Don't be scared to get a little dirty. That means getting on your hands and knees to look for maker's marks, opening drawers, flipping chairs over if you have to, or crawling underneath tables to find a signature (or some sort of context clues, such as an original price tag).

Visit the sale *more* than once

ESTATE SALES

Level: Intermediate to advanced

Minimum time requirement: 1 hour (more if you get there early to wait in line)

Negotiation Expected? No (Some estate sales will allow you to place bids on higher-ticket items, —and if it doesn't sell by the final day, they'll generally accept your offer)

You know how there are Disney people? Those folks who buy yearly passes every January, have mouse-eared stick figures on their car, and can tell you where every hidden Mickey in the Magic Kingdom is? Well, there are also estate sale people. They, too, wake up at the crack of dawn to experience a whole new world, albeit one that can't be easily accessed via a fairy godmother.

If you go to estate sales often enough, like I do, you'll start to notice the same group of people at almost every sale: There are the lookie-loos (who just want to see the house), the neighbors (who want to get a look at the renovations in person), and the collectors (who are in the market for something very specific, such as records, angel figurines, or military memorabilia). And then there are the dealers, who are likely eyeing the same things as you and therefore must be taken out at all costs—by which I mean you have to get on "the list" before them.

Some estate sales will have a list—a sheet of paper that's stuck to the front door the day before the sale and numbered—to ensure that shoppers come inside in an orderly fashion. To find out if there's a list and whether you can get on it, call the company hosting the sale beforehand (or, frankly, just drive to the house the day prior to see if there's a list on the door).

The sales without a list are the most cutthroat. If you aren't able to sign up beforehand, I recommend arriving at an estate sale as early as 6 a.m. for a sale that begins at 9 a.m. I might sound like a total nut (I am), but I've been burned in the past. I once attended a killer estate sale at a huge home on the water. I called the company the day before, to determine if there was a list. There wasn't, so I arrived bright and early at 6 a.m. the next day. Imagine my surprise when I saw that someone had created her own makeshift list, against the rules of the company. The sale began at 9 a.m., so I stood at the front door and waited for 3 hours as people began to line up behind me. And guess who strolled up at 8:45 a.m. and walked herself to the front of the line? I am sad to report that I didn't stick up for myself then, but it served as a good reminder of the importance of making friends (and not being afraid to throw an elbow if someone cuts in front of you).

I like to think of myself as an estate sale master. I have a very specific ritual I follow, which goes a little something like this:

ONE: Seek out the sales: EstateSales.net is the holy grail of estate sale sites. I check it at least once a day, to see the dates, times, and photos of upcoming sales. Some companies will only post a handful of photos, but others will post hundreds. If you don't see a specific item pictured, don't let this deter you: Even some estate sale staffers don't always know what they have, so they won't necessarily upload photos of every item in the house. I once found an Issey Miyake blouse at a sale for $2 (retail price: $525), tucked into a bathroom closet.

TWO: Do some internet sleuthing: I used to be an investigative reporter, and those skills still come in handy.

When I'm looking at photos of upcoming sales, I spend hours examining what's in the background and foreground to be sure I don't miss anything. I will also search for the homes on real estate websites prior to a sale to get an idea of how the house is laid out: If I'm going to the sale for a specific item, this allows me to know exactly where to go once I'm in the house.

THREE: Visit the sale more than once: Day one of a sale is the most competitive, and if you see something you can't live without, you should absolutely buy it. (I refer to this as the "no man left behind" rule. I've experienced the loss of a vintage item many times due to the faulty logic that I could come back for it later.) But if you see something that's above your budget, go back the next day to try for it. Days two and three usually come with reduced prices—25 percent off on day two, 35 percent off on day three, that kind of thing. Plus, I find that I usually have a clearer head once I'm familiar with the territory, so I might even come across items I didn't see the day before.

FOUR: Get the inside scoop on where the items are heading next: It's rare for an estate sale company to sell all of its merchandise during a sale, which may leave you wondering where all the stuff goes after the final day. Most companies have relationships with specific charities and will donate unsold merchandise to an area charity shop or thrift store. Get to know the people working the sale, and they might tell you where the unsold items will be headed once the sale has ended.

TIP! If you see an item that you love but it's out of your price range, don't be afraid to see if the estate sale company is taking bids. (They often will, particularly for higher-priced pieces, such as valuable art.)

AUCTIONS

Level: Advanced
Minimum time requirement: 1 hour
Negotiation expected? No way—you'll be bidding instead

If places to shop for vintage were ranked like Taco Bell hot sauces, auctions would be diablo. Live auctions, especially, are not for those with a weak palate.

There's always a person shouting (the auctioneer) and a crowd of people clamoring and competing for the goods—and then there's the heart-pumping adrenaline that might cause you to go way over budget in your quest to win.

In layman's terms, an auction is a sale held either in person or virtually in which goods are sold to the highest bidder. Once bidding begins, you have a limited time (at a live auction, literally minutes) to place your bid, with bids increasing until, basically, no one can stomach taking it any further. The spoils go to the victors, and the victors are those with the highest budgets.

I prefer the virtual experience, wherein no one can see you bidding on a 1950s console with one hand while shoveling a Popeyes chicken sandwich in your mouth with the other.

My best tips for auctions are the same whether they're online or in person: Be patient and stick to a budget. When bidding online, try to wait until a few minutes before the item ends to place your bid. (This will give you the best chance of winning. If you place your bid too early, competitors will have enough time to outbid you.)

The budget thing cannot be emphasized enough. Most of us get deeply carried away by the thrill of winning. I have been known to spend way too much on something simply because my competitive instincts kicked in. That's pretty much the whole point of an auction, so stay strong! Don't be like me. Decide on your budget before you go, and don't bid above it.

TIP! Bring a friend if you're worried you might go overboard when it comes time to bid. Having someone there who can provide a gut check (and a hard elbow if you start to spend way too much in the heat of the moment) will hold you accountable.

Get Out of Town

ONCE YOU'VE BEEN BITTEN BY THE THRIFTING BUG, you'll eventually want to venture outside your comfort zone to treasure hunt in new territories. I've been fortunate enough to take several road trips around the country, hitting up flea markets, estate sales, antiques shops, and thrift stores along the way. What I've learned is that every part of the country has its own aesthetic, one that's often reflected in the merchandise available there. Here are the regions that stand out to me most.

SOUTH FLORIDA

Hollywood Regency and glam, baby. South Florida is chock-full of Lucite, rattan, chinoiserie, and all the wicker you could possibly dream of. Word to the wise: Many of the thrift stores in this region (everywhere from West Palm Beach to Sarasota) are priced more like a high-end antiques store, so don't go expecting to find a bargain.

MICHIGAN

Beautiful examples of Mid-Century Modern design abound in and around Detroit, which was one of America's most powerful cities in its heyday (roughly 1920–1940). The arts and culture of the city are immortalized in many of the area's homes. Search estate sales in and around the Motor City and you'll see what I mean: Expect Hans Wegner bookcases, and tons of great abstract art.

THE SOUTHWEST

The Southwest is a big region, and it's tough to narrow down the best vintage shopping to one city or state. Everywhere from Phoenix, Arizona, to Albuquerque, New Mexico, has been influenced by the environment and local culture, including Native Americans, who have long called this area home and shaped its art and design aesthetic. Look for lots of turquoise jewelry, terra-cotta and clay vessels, beautiful sculptures, and large-scale canvases in muted hues that mirror the local terrain.

PALM SPRINGS

Similar to south Florida, the thrift shops and antiques malls that dot the California desert call to mind a bygone era when glasses of Scotch were consumed in the office, cigarettes were smoked onstage, and glitz was the name of the game. Mid-Century Mod is huge in Palm Springs even today, so you might find some of that, as well as local art and vintage clothing. Because Palm Springs is a hot tourist spot, thrifts here tend to be pricier.

RHODE ISLAND

Here's a little secret: Any area that's home to a stellar design school is probably also home to stellar thrift shopping. That's because young artists are, well, artsy: They wear cool clothes, have quirky housewares, and often head to thrifts to off-load their own items, including half-finished paintings or sketches they got sick of having in their studio space. The area in and around the Rhode Island School of Design is proof positive of this.

UPSTATE NEW YORK

You'll find a lot of traditional pieces that are pure Americana, such as Federalist mirrors, stunning old portraits, vintage leather suitcases that can be stacked and used as tables, and many more classic pieces. The Hudson Valley (think: Woodstock) in particular is brimming with upscale antiques shops.

TEXAS

Texas has long been teeming with glitz, glam, and pageantry that's often on display in its state fairs and rodeos—and also translates to home furnishings and fashion. So perhaps it's unsurprising that there are some pretty terrific thrift shops in the Houston and Dallas areas, as well as some of the smaller towns sprinkled throughout the Lone Star State. After all, this is where oil bigwigs and other society types have settled down for years, donating their castoffs—fringed Roberto Cavalli jackets, Hermès saddles, jet-black wicker peacock chairs—to local charity shops before buying all-new furniture and accessories to redecorate.

VIRGINIA

Best Flea Markets in the U.S.

FLEA MARKETS CROP UP ALL OVER THE UNITED STATES throughout the year. But there are some biggies—the kind frequented by both big-name interior designers and furniture company staffers. (Where else do you think they get all the inspo for their new stuff?) Here's a list of the biggest and best.

BRIMFIELD ANTIQUE FLEA MARKET

Location: Brimfield, Massachusetts
Date: May, July, and September

This truly is the mother of all antique markets and consists of 20 privately owned shows spread out over a series of fields. You won't make it through everything in one day, so don't even try. Instead, come armed with a vague list of what you're looking for, and be prepared to leave with so much more than that. (You should probably snag an apple cider doughnut, too, for fuel. You're gonna need it.)

BROOKLYN FLEA

Location: New York City
Date: Weekly

Brooklyn's largest flea market has expanded out of its original neighborhood, now encompassing several locations—Williamsburg, DUMBO, the Lower East Side, and Chelsea—and offering more than one day per week to shop. That means there's plenty of opportunity to look for vintage records, posters, and clothing. Also, there are food trucks, so you can make a day of it.

ROUND TOP

Location: Round Top, Texas
Date: Multiple shows in winter, spring, and fall

Round Top's antique weeks (held three times a year) are a rite of passage for vintage fiends. If you don't happen to be one of the 90 people who live in this quaint Texas town, you'll have to drive quite a ways to find it, but it's pretty magical. This market is on the pricier side, so don't go expecting to find tons of buried treasure. The upside is that the sellers here know what they have, which means they've already done the work for you. Expect tent after tent of beautiful things expertly curated by the discerning eyes of top vintage dealers. Multiple shows, taking up over 20 miles, comprise this event, so set aside a couple of days to take it all in.

ROSE BOWL FLEA MARKET

Location: Pasadena, California
Date: Second Sunday of every month

Legendary in every way, the Rose Bowl is almost worth it just to get inspo from all the great outfits worn by other shoppers. You'll find a lot of fun housewares and fashions, but bring exact change for vendors who only accept cash. This is a particularly good market for vintage denim, which is incredibly pricey and hard to find elsewhere.

ALAMEDA POINT ANTIQUES FAIRE

Location: Alameda, California
Date: First Sunday of every month

Set against the backdrop of the San Francisco skyline, this is a true vintage show (all items sold here are required to be 20 years of age or older), and there's plenty to pick from with more than 800 vendors. There's also a separate Alameda Vintage Fashion Faire, which is great for the sartorial set. The indoor event includes more than 70 booths selling vintage men's and women's fashions, jewelry, couture, and every hat or bag your heart could desire.

RENNINGER'S ANTIQUE & COLLECTORS EXTRAVA-GANZA

In Pennsylvania: Kutztown and Adamstown
In Florida: Melbourne and Mount Dora
Date: A few times a year

I have been frequenting Renninger's in Mount Dora, Florida, since I was just a girl. Three times a year, dealers from across the country set up shop in an expansive field (on a steepish hill, which I assume is the highest point in Florida), selling everything from buckets of sea glass to Mid-Century furnishings. I always leave with a carload (or rented vanload) of stuff. It's also really fun to say the word "extravaganza" in a fancy accent for a weekend. The Pennsylvania markets are equally packed; fitting with the location, you'll find fewer coastal accessories and more well-made furniture. Unlike some of the bigger markets (Roundtop, Alameda), you can find some really great deals here, but you'll still spend hours shopping.

TIP! If you can, buy an early-bird pass to a flea market. Some will allow shoppers to pay more to enter a few hours early. The discounts won't be as great as on the final day, but you'll get first pick of all the goodies!

PART TWO

HOW TO SHOP

NOW THAT YOU'RE PREPARED, LET'S TALK ABOUT what to do once you're actually out in the wild. What should you look for? What should you buy? What's a valuable diamond in the rough, and what should you ditch?

Beyond any specific needs and wants on your list, there are a few key ways to filter your shopping experience so you don't end up totally overwhelmed and wasting lots of time. Considering materials, staple items, labels, and timeless trends will help you sort through the junk and feel confident that you've scored something good.

MURANO GLASS

COTTAGECORE

ABSTRACT FACES

RATTAN, WICKER, & CANE

BLACK & WHITE

PLASTER

MURANO GLASS

Trendspotting

IT'S BEEN SAID THAT EVERYTHING COMES BACK IN STYLE EVENTUALLY. One of my favorite things about perusing the catalogs of big-name brands is that I always spot at least a dozen items that are modeled after vintage pieces I've had and loved. And the original is typically better than the riff on it.

Here are a few past trends that have proven to be quite timeless.

MURANO GLASS

The craft of glassmaking has been honed over generations on the Italian island of Murano. The resulting pieces of heavy (and, let's face it, unbearably sexy) Murano glass lamps, vases, and bowls are not only highly collectible, but also always feel relevant, design-wise. (It is glass, after all, so it kind of goes with anything.)

The name doesn't refer to a brand, though legit pieces might be stamped with a "Murano" sticker or signature. If you don't see any sort of mark or sticker, you can tell Murano is the real deal by looking for imperfections, such as air bubbles within the glass or pontil marks (indentations that are a result of the glassmaking process).

Image at top: The mushroom lamp—so named for its cheeky shape—is an iconic and highly collectible piece of art glass. Also an estate sale find, this particular piece cost me $125.

Image at bottom: This heavy, black Murano bowl (which I sourced for $12 at an estate sale) serves as the perfect catchall for matchbooks or jewelry.

PLASTER

Crisp, white plaster has recently found its way into everything from fireplace mantles to dining room tables, but it's certainly nothing new. In the late 1980s throughout the '90s, artist John Dickinson used the material to cast tables and chairs in a whimsical way, so that they took on the shapes of animal hooves, or looked like they were draped in a blanket. Though the look was over the top originally, a piece of white plaster furniture today works for both the minimalists and maximalists (hi, I'm Virginia) among us.

OPPOSITE: I found this trompe l'œil table base at a thrift store for $5. Though it was sold with a glass top, I let the store keep the piece of glass and instead painted the base a crisp, chalky white. The resulting piece calls to mind the work of John Dickinson, with similar tables retailing for hundreds, if not thousands, of dollars.

ABSTRACT FACES

The trend toward single-line and Matisse-like faces has jumped from the canvas to the housewares department. The best way to replicate this style of vintage goods is to look for outsider art (pieces created by self-taught artists). Bowls or paintings made in a childhood art class, for instance, often have a tendency to look on trend.

OPPOSITE An iron John Risley chair (found at an estate sale for $50) takes up residence in my backyard, adding whimsy to an other-wise traditional space.

On Your Mark

So, what is a maker's mark anyway? Think of it as a trademark. It can help you identify who made a piece, where it came from, and even how much it might be worth. Over time, you'll be able to identify and verify logos, signatures, and other markings. But until then, use your trusty phone to google marks and signatures before you buy.

Here's where to find them:

Furniture: Check drawers and the underside or the back of a piece to find any stamp or tag that might be hiding. If you don't see anything, look for a guild or association mark or the name of a store (Sears Roebuck & Co., for instance), which could help you launch your search. You might also see a serial number, which you can search on a furniture company's website. (If it's an important piece, there should be more info about it.)

Porcelain and pottery: Check the bottom. A piece of china will often bear two marks: one beneath the glaze—labeling the factory that produced it—and the second above the glaze, indicating the artist. Warning: Marks on china are some of the most imitated in the world, so there's always the possibility that something is a copy.

Art and sculpture: With paintings, always check the corners, as well as the back of a canvas. Signatures on a piece of sculpture are harder to find; they may be on the base of a piece or somewhere on the body. Look everywhere.

Crystal: The most well-known crystal manufacturers usually etch their name or logo into an inconspicuous area of the crystal itself. Use a magnifying glass to check the stem or the bottom.

RATTAN, WICKER, AND CANE

Being a Florida native, my firm belief is that wicker and rattan can never really go out of style, but it's a material that's transitioned from a sunroom-only Palm Beach essential to a California cool-girl must-have. When mixed with other design elements, rattan doesn't have to read "vacation rental." Paired with soft colors, it looks earthy and can even read as modern in some spaces.

ABOVE: These 1960s wicker frogs abound at Florida estate sales, and they happen to be a Hollywood Regency–collector's dream. Here, I paired mine with a Francois Carre sunburst chair (a $40 estate sale find that retails for much more).

COTTAGECORE

The frills, chintz, toile, and skirted tables of the late 1980s and early '90s are back in a big way. Often referred to as "grandmillennial" or "trad," this is one of the easiest aesthetics to find in a thrift store. Just look for patterns and embellishments: anything embroidered; vintage quilts to layer on a bed; lace tablecloths; gingham napkins; checkered accents to layer on bedside tables; and vintage portraits.

ABOVE: Checkerboard is a hallmark of cottagecore style. I found this harlequin-esque quilt at an estate sale, and use it to jazz up a beige console and inject color and pattern into an already vibrant space.

Everything
comes back
in style.

MIRRORS

FIGURAL SCULPTURES

LIGHT FIXTURES

OUTDOOR ACCESSORIES

OUTDOOR ACCESSORIES

BUSTS

PORTRAITS

OYSTER PLATES

The Go-Tos

WE'VE ALREADY ESTABLISHED THAT IT'S IMPORTANT to keep an open mind when shopping vintage. That being said, there are a handful of items that are always worth looking for, mainly because they tend to be pricey when not bought secondhand. If you're crunched for time and don't feel like spending hours in a store, do a quick hunt for the following items.

OYSTER PLATES

Oyster plates (so named because they are built to hold the bivalves) are not only very rare but also very pricey, ranging from the hundreds to the thousands. If you see one at the thrift store, snatch it up. They are supremely special, not necessarily for their function—How many of us are actually eating raw oysters off fancy china, anyway?—but for their unique design and intricate details. Oyster plates look especially chic hung in a grouping on a wall.

VINTAGE PORTRAITS

Not your grandpa? Not a problem. Older portraits lend so much character (literally) to a wall. Alas, antique portraiture tends to be expensive at high-end shops, and most of us don't have the budget to commission a portrait of our loved ones or ourselves. So if you happen upon a great painting—of, well, anyone—at the thrift store and it's within your budget, snap it up. Even if the old man on the canvas isn't a distant relative, he might still be a worthy addition to your wall.

ABOVE **Vintage posters by well-known artists are also affordable ways to inject portraiture into your home.**

LIGHT FIXTURES

BELOW **Vintage Lucite** will probably never go out of style, and thanks to being clear, it goes with nearly anything.

If you've ever gone lamp or chandelier shopping, you know that lighting is pricey! Fortunately, lamps, chandeliers, and sconces are all readily available at secondhand shops and estate sales for reasonable prices. They're just begging to be plugged in to light up your life.

ABSTRACT SCULPTURES

I have a soft spot for anything figural, so I snatch up anything and everything modeled after the human body. In general, I'm drawn to abstract pieces, which feel much more one of a kind than something made in a factory. I've found many interesting figural sculptures over the years, from artist-made originals to studio pieces that were in production in the 1970s. They provide interesting shapes and lines, and scale to any tableau and can be blended with all types of styles, so keep them at the top of your list.

BUSTS

Heads are another favorite of mine to collect (something about displaying someone else's face in your home, y'know?), and there are so many out there to find. It's fun to mix: A collection of classic Grecian busts, Art Deco faces, and even artist-made masks can all live in harmony.

MIRRORS

Statement mirrors are ridiculously expensive. You know the ones—begging to be used for an OOTD (outfit of the day, if you're not in the know) Instagram shot. Luckily, thrift stores are full of great mirrors, and most of them are in good shape. Don't worry about the quality of the glass; that's an easy (and fairly inexpensive) fix. Instead, look for interesting shapes—circles, full-length rectangles, or even curved, sexy mirrors that could turn your master bathroom from just OK to "Oh baby."

OUTDOOR ACCESSORIES

Planters, garden stools, and outdoor iron furniture are all extremely expensive at big-name chain stores and high-end design shops. Vintage items (particularly those scooped up at a thrift store or estate sale) are less expensive, with the natural patina that comes with age and works perfectly in an outdoor setting.

OPPOSITE **I've found several animal-shaped garden stools at thrift stores and estate sales. Even though it has a few chips, this antique elephant stool has so much character.**

Always
shop with an
open mind

FEEL GOOD FACTOR

Did you know that the EPA estimates that the average person throws away 81 pounds of clothing per year? The fast-fashion problem has also extended to our housewares, with the agency estimating that 9 million tons of furniture are tossed every single year.

From an environmental standpoint, the way we shop for things today is incredibly wasteful. And from a financial standpoint, quick and cheap means we aren't investing in well-made items that will last. One of the most beautiful things about a vintage habit is that it is a pretty guilt-free way to outfit both your home and yourself. Rather than shopping for new things, which increases the demand for more new things, you're purchasing items that have already been used and loved—and are probably a bit better for it.

Donating to and buying from thrift stores not only helps keep items out of a landfill but also gives them a second life. Plus, many thrift stores put their profits toward creating jobs in the local community or funding organizations that focus on everything from animal welfare to domestic violence—a win-win situation.

Material World

ANOTHER WAY TO MAKE THINGS EVEN EASIER on yourself is to look for certain materials—the higher the material quality, the more well made the piece. Here are the materials I always keep my eyes peeled for.

MARBLE

From the ancient Romans to the Kardashians, the wealthy and powerful have been styling with marble for eons, displaying it in the form of fireplaces, tables, sculptures, and tile work. Even if you don't have Kim K. money, you can still incorporate marble in either small (abstract sculptures) or large (dining tables) doses.

OPPOSITE: I found this deep-burgundy marble table at a thrift store for $35. It's such a heavy piece that the staffers weren't able to lift the tabletop onto the base, so the two pieces were in different corners of the shop. The weight probably had something to do with the low price as well—who wants to lug that thing home? (Spoiler alert: me-e-e-e-e.)

LEFT **The brass legs on the table mirror the brass frame on the print, and the brass lamp. Don't be afraid to really go for it and use multiple pieces cast from the same materials in one space.**

BRASS

Brass is one of those materials that just looks luxe. It adds shine to any space and mixes in well with other metals. Here's a little tip: If you find a piece of brass furniture, check underneath for a Sarreid label, which is exceptionally high-end brand and still in production. Their vintage pieces (like chests and coffee tables) were often clad in brass and are highly collectible (and just plain attractive). Even if it's not Sarreid, brass anything is still a worthy buy. Too much and it can read a little too "glam," but a small dose adds just the right amount of glam.

OPPOSITE: These brass and pink velvet Milo Baughman–style barstools are one of my favorite finds. I bought them at a used furniture shop for $35. (This particular store is run by a man who buys all the unsold merchandise from estate sales once the sale is over, so he's constantly getting in new inventory, and it's always fun.)

LUCITE

Lucite, acrylic, and plexiglass are all high-quality materials favored by designers for a reason: They are expensive AF to produce. To create Lucite tables, chairs, trunks, and sculptures requires that sheets of acrylic be cut, heated, and bent into shape. So know that if you find an amazing (that is, heavy and thick) accessory or piece of furniture made of Lucite, it's probably a good find.

LEATHER

Leather really does get better with age, so it makes sense to buy it when you see it at an affordable price. I always look for leather skirts, jackets, and furniture when I run into a thrift store or antiques mall, as it's an expensive material you could never otherwise find for a great price.

PLASTER

Plaster has been having a major moment in design of late, and I think it's because it's so sculptural and works well with so many aesthetics, from Scandinavian minimal to Palm Beach punchy. I happen to think it looks best white. You can also easily make just about anything look like plaster with a can of matte-white chalk paint.

ONE HUNDRED SEASHELLS   HAROLD FEINSTEIN
Pond Lake River Sea

BURL

I have such a thing for burl. Any time I see it, I snatch it up. This wood actually comes from a growth on a tree (gross, right?), but the inside of said growth is distorted in a really beautiful, tortoiseshell way—proof not to judge a book by its cover.

Burl first became popular in the 1920s, so you'll notice it used in a lot of Art Deco designs. It was at its height in the '70s, so vintage shops are a great place to find it.

ABOVE: I love burl in all its iterations, even the fake stuff (like laminate). This laminate "burl" armoire, which I purchased for $150 at an estate sale, serves as my bar cabinet.

A *little dose* of tacky is *a-okay* with me

How to Clean Secondhand

If you notice a small stain on something, don't freak. It could still be a worthy buy. In fact, a lot of stains are surprisingly easy to remove, as long as you know a few tricks and use a little elbow grease.

Water Rings on Wood: If you're dealing with ring stains on wood, put a few dollops of mayo on a paper towel, press it into the water ring, let it sit for a minute, and then gently rub the ring. This should do the trick. Your house (or wherever you happen to be when cleaning said water rings) might smell like potato salad for a little while, but the rings will vanish. Win-win in my book.

Sticker marks: Goo Gone is a good investment if you thrift a lot. Most thrift items have sticky price tags on them, and the residue can be a pain to remove. Goo Gone works well, but if you don't have it handy, a little rubbing alcohol or even actual alcohol (vodka or something similarly clear) will help loosen adhesive.

Sharpie: A lot of thrift stores eschew price tags for straight up drawing on a piece with marker. Rubbing alcohol on a Q-tip works wonders. If that doesn't remove it, break out the big gun: nail polish remover.

Stains: Believe it or not, a stained piece of fabric (on a chair, couch, or even a blanket) doesn't have to be a deal-breaker. In fact, stains on upholstery are generally easy to remove. Mix two cups of warm water with a quarter cup of white vinegar and a teaspoon of dish detergent. Use a soft-bristled brush (a clean toothbrush, even) to rub the stain out and blot it dry with a clean towel. A cotton swab dipped in rubbing alcohol can also do the trick, if the stain is ink-based.

Stinky stuff: Weird smells kind of come with the territory. If you come across a particularly noxious odor, try rubbing baking soda on the item. It will neutralize the odor via some strange and magical chemical reaction—like it does when you keep an open container of the stuff in your fridge.

When to Just Say No

SMALL STAINS ARE ONE THING. RIPS, TEARS, AND CRACKS, HOWEVER? Those are entering into make-or-break (literally) territory. There are other reasons to pass on an item, too—like having nowhere to put it. Here's a handy guide on knowing when to turn your back on peer pressure (or, y'know, that voice inside your head that says, "Buy it!") and just say no.

IF IT'S DAMAGED BEYOND REPAIR

Stained silk? Hard pass. A table or chair that's missing a leg? It's gonna be a no for me. When shopping vintage furniture, look for solid wood, rather than veneer or particleboard, and check for any peeling or splintering. Leather sometimes looks better a little worn or cracked, but be sure you're OK with that before forking over your hard-earned cash for a distressed couch. When looking at metal or brass pieces, try to stay away from anything tarnished or pitted. (Brasso works wonders, if you're willing to put some elbow grease into making over something that's a little worse for wear.)

IF YOU DON'T HAVE THE SPACE

I have been guilty of buying things that I have no space for, just because I was in the mood to buy something. This is bad. This is the opposite of what we want to do when we go vintage shopping, and it really contributes to the whole stuff-in-landfills problem that we should all work harder to fix. OK, off my soapbox.

IF IT'S A BREAKABLE PIECE THAT'S ALREADY CHIPPED

While it's possible to fix chipped or broken pottery, it's impossible to make it look like the original. And fixing broken glassware is not a DIY I personally care to take on. (I really don't have the talent to add glassblowing to my résumé.) Examine pottery closely for chips before you buy!

IF IT DOESN'T WORK

Often, thrift stores will check if an electronic item is operable before placing it on the floor, but don't be afraid to ask if you can borrow an outlet to plug something in. While you might tell yourself you'll get a broken lamp or light fixture rewired, I promise you, you won't.

All of the above being said, I fully embrace the Japanese idea of wabi sabi, which is to accept things as they are or even embrace them because of their flaws. Some imperfections are OK, but if it's not functional or the imperfections are all you see, I'd suggest leaving it behind.

Don't chase trends. Find *your own* style and let it evolve with time.

LEE REYNOLDS

AUSTIN PRODUCTIONS

KNOLL

FITZ & FLOYD

CHRISTIAN DIOR

KNOLL

KNOLL

MAITLAND SMITH

Labels to Look For

I KNOW WHAT YOU'RE THINKING: CHRISTIAN DIOR? AT A THRIFT STORE? No way. But I've spotted several pieces by the below brands at thrift stores across the country, so I know for a fact they're out there. All of the following brands are known for well-designed, unique pieces that stand the test of time. (And the thrift store prices are sure to be a tiny fraction of the cost of the piece elsewhere.) If you spot items with these labels, snatch them up.

AUSTIN PRODUCTIONS

Founded in 1950s Brooklyn, Austin was a museum reproduction company specializing in art collections of Egyptian, Greek, Roman, Asian, African, and contemporary sculpture. Their pieces are noteworthy in that many are signed and dated, making it easy to identify a time period. While they aren't super valuable, they do sell on the secondary market for $100–$500. (And many of their older pieces happen to be very on trend.)

Look For: Small, artful sculptures that look like they're made of plaster

CHRISTIAN DIOR

Founded in 1946, Christian Dior remains one of the most revered fashion houses on Earth. Synonymous with luxury, even a 30-year-old Dior blazer or champagne glass will stand the test of time.

Look For: Dior has made trench coats, floor-length capes, gowns, and blazers for decades, and I've actually found all of the above at thrift stores. The best way to see if an item is made by Christian Dior—or any fashion house, for that matter—is to check the tag, either on the back of the neck or inside a garment, near the bottom of the hem. Dior has also produced housewares, so look for branded playing cards, flatware, wineglasses, luggage, and even game sets like backgammon.

ABOVE **There was no tag on this Dior cape I thrifted for $10, but it was easily identifiable by the silk CD logo that lines the inside.**

LEE REYNOLDS BURR

As the director of Vanguard Studios, artist Lee Reynolds oversaw a number of paintings that now bear his name. They sell for hundreds—sometimes thousands—on the secondary market. Note that most of these paintings will be signed "Lee Reynolds," but only the works signed "Lee Reynolds Burr" were created solely by the artist, making those especially rare and valuable.

Look For: Large-scale 1980s and '90s acrylic or oil paintings

BELOW **A thrifted Lee Reynolds makes itself at home with other vintage odds and ends.**

FITZ AND FLOYD

While this company still churns out decorative ceramic tableware and accessories, some of their best stuff is vintage. It's almost always marked—so check for a sticker, their logo, or an "FF" underneath—and definitely fun and kitschy.

Look For: Small items, such as animals, tissue box holders, platters, and the like

MAITLAND-SMITH

Maitland-Smith has been in the business of making beautiful things for decades. While they still create furniture and accessories, some of their most interesting— and, ironically, on trend—pieces are vintage. In the 1980s and '90s, in particular, they often used stone to create pieces of furniture that are curved, bold, and sexy.

Look For: Ginger jars, stone furniture, and geometric/Art Deco–style boxes

KNOLL

A lot of big-name furniture designers and architects have created pieces for Knoll, including Harry Bertoia, Ludwig Mies van der Rohe, and Eero Saarinen, to name a few. Familiarize yourself with Knoll designs, and you'll know how to spot one out in the wild. Always check for a "Knoll" tag underneath, although the absence of one doesn't mean the piece isn't authentic.

Look For: Marble-top tulip tables, curved chrome chairs, anything that manages to look both sculptural and industrial, and leather office chairs

Friends with Benefits

The world of collecting can be competitive (trust me, that little old lady in line for the same estate sale as you is not as innocent as she looks!), but it can also be collaborative. Don't be afraid to chat up the "regulars" you always spot shopping or the workers and dealers at your favorite shops. Making friends with the people working at your local spots means they'll probably tell you when they get a great shipment in. Getting to know other local dealers and collectors works similarly: They can help you find specific, hard-to-find pieces you've been lusting after for years.

Sourcing can be unpredictable, but if a particular booth at an antiques gallery always catches your eye, it means the dealer's eye meets your design vision. Reach out to them to see if they have a warehouse you could shop or if they'd be willing to hunt down a particular piece for you. They'll likely find something else you'll swoon over.

Friendly fellow antiquers can come in especially handy when you're both shopping at a faraway flea market. If one of them has a truck or van, they might be willing to haul some of your finds for a small fee, which is a lot easier than investing in your own truck or rental. It takes a village!

PART THREE

HOW TO STYLE

THE TRUE STORY OF A HOME DEVELOPS with time and patience. A room full of matchy-matchy, brand-new things looks decorated, and while some people prefer that look, I wouldn't consider it styled. Developing a style is a continuous process of layering things that add history, panache, interest, and personality to a space.

I have a lot of tried-and-true tips for styling a room—ways to add balance and interest, all that fun stuff—that I'll get into in this section. But rules are, of course, meant to be broken, so please use these only as loose guidelines and do what feels best for you.

Before we get to the tips, let's talk about that all-too-elusive design skill that's the foundation for everything else: having confidence.

Think like a Designer

THE REAL JOY IN DECORATING COMES FROM FILLING YOUR SPACE with what you love. But maybe you don't know how to take the myriad pieces you love and have them live in harmony. No worries. You'll get there.

We talked about the importance of preparation before you go shopping. Similarly, with styling, it's a good idea to get in the right headspace. Here's what helps me.

COLLECT INSPIRATION

Whether you use Pinterest, save images on Instagram, or do things the old-fashioned way (take screenshots of anything interesting and save them to your desktop until you can no longer remember what your background was), cataloging rooms you've seen and loved will undoubtedly help you outfit your own space.

Once you've built up a solid selection of inspo shots, make notes about what you love about them. Is it the mix of colors and textures? The juxtaposition of an over-size painting with a slightly smaller table? Rather than trying to replicate your inspiration, use it as a template.

Maybe you pinned a living room with green chairs, a chrome-legged dining table, and dark walls. Write down those materials and colors, along with your necessities (oversize painting, dining table, six chairs), and use it as a shopping list. You might not find a chrome-legged dining table, but maybe you'll find a chrome lamp you could use in the room and still achieve the same mix of materials and colors you loved in the inspiration photo.

LET FORM FOLLOW FUNCTION

Before decorating any space, first take into account the function of the room: Will you need to work in that room and should you therefore make space for a desk? Will it include a TV, and if so, where should it go and what's the best seating arrangement to view it? Will you be eating in this room? Does the room have enough storage, or does it need a piece of furniture to help house toys and odds and ends? Having a beautiful space is great, but you need to be able to live in it.

TAKE NOTE OF WHAT YOU ALREADY HAVE

In the interest of saving money (and time and energy), try to make use of what you have. Let's say you have a tufted brown leather couch you aren't ready to replace, but you're at a loss when it comes to making it feel fresh. Take ideas from others. Just search "tufted brown leather couch" on Pinterest and Google to see how others have decorated with a similar piece. The algorithms will, of course, offer you more inspiration than you could possibly handle, but you'll eventually see something that makes you think, Hmm, why didn't I think of styling it that way? A simple refresh can make a big difference.

Similarly, if there's something in the room you don't love but can't get rid of, think of ways to embrace it. If it's an old radiator, add a slim piece of marble or wood to the top and turn it into a table. If it's an industrial pipe, make it a focal point by painting it a bright color. Hate the floors but not ready to commit to new ones? Layer interesting rugs all over the space before you add any furniture.

CHOOSE YOUR MOOD

Do you want the space to feel bright and modern or layered and cozy? The desired mood determines the direction your design takes, starting with the wall color (or wallpaper, if that's more your speed) and rugs or flooring. Note that you don't need to stick with a single mood for the entire home. One room might be more pragmatic and material-led, while the room next door is whimsical, playful, and eclectic. In my own home, I went with a hyperfeminine-but-Millennial look in the master bedroom. One of the guest bedrooms, meanwhile, looks like an old sailor lives in it. Then the formal living room is a chic salon—the type of place where you'd sip a Sazerac by the fire (or a LaCroix while listening to Taylor Swift). When you're out shopping, be sure to channel the mood of the room you're styling.

OPPOSITE **An auction find, this counter-weight lamp offers a dose of clean-lined minimalism when paired with more romantic pieces.**

LET THERE BE LIGHT

The light in a space is so, so important. If the room you're designing already has great light via big windows, you're in luck. If not, it's time to buy some lighting fixtures. Think of lighting as a way to guide the eye around the room. Which aspects will need a spotlight, such as a sconce for paintings or a floor light next to a chair for reading? Does the room need more central light, such as a ceiling pendant light? Good lighting makes a huge difference, and as I mentioned in the shopping section of this book, light fixtures and lamps are great things to buy vintage.

BE PATIENT

This is hard for me—I'm not a patient person—but sometimes you just have to wait it out until you find the perfect piece or come up with the perfect idea for finishing a room. When I needed a desk for my home office, I searched for months but couldn't find anything that spoke to me. So I bought an affordable IKEA piece to use as a stand-in until I can find the piece that's just right. Remember, styling is an ongoing process. Try not to rush to "get it done."

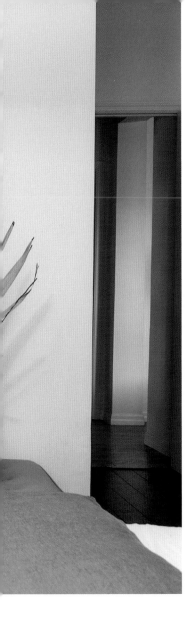

DON'T OVERTHINK IT

At the same time, pondering every single item in a room will slow down your timeline and probably make the space kind of boring. It's fun to have some whimsy and spontaneity involved, even if the results aren't perfect. One of the best parts of aging, in my opinion, is learning to let go of what others might think or of striving for perfection. If you're like me—read: a perfectionist who is never really satisfied—you'll never get to 100 percent and perfect. And that's OK, because 80 percent done can be just as beautiful.

STEP OUTSIDE YOUR COMFORT ZONE

I often hear, "I wish I could pull that off," when I post a hypercolorful room or share a funky outfit on Instagram. The truth is, anyone can pull anything off; you just have to be willing to try! (What's the worst that could happen?) If you don't usually experiment with color but find yourself drawn to the punchy patterns in a room you saw in the pages of *Domino*, try it in small doses: Add a few checkered boxes or an abstract painting to a neutral room. Over time, you can take more and more "risks" in your space. There is no right or wrong when it comes to your personal style, and you can always make changes, so don't be afraid to mix things up.

GO WITH YOUR GUT

Trusting your gut is really the key when it comes to being confident in your design decisions. Try new things—place an oversize table lamp on the floor, throw a rug over a couch—and live with it for a couple of days. If you still love it, your instincts were on point. I find that when I listen to my gut, I usually love the outcome.

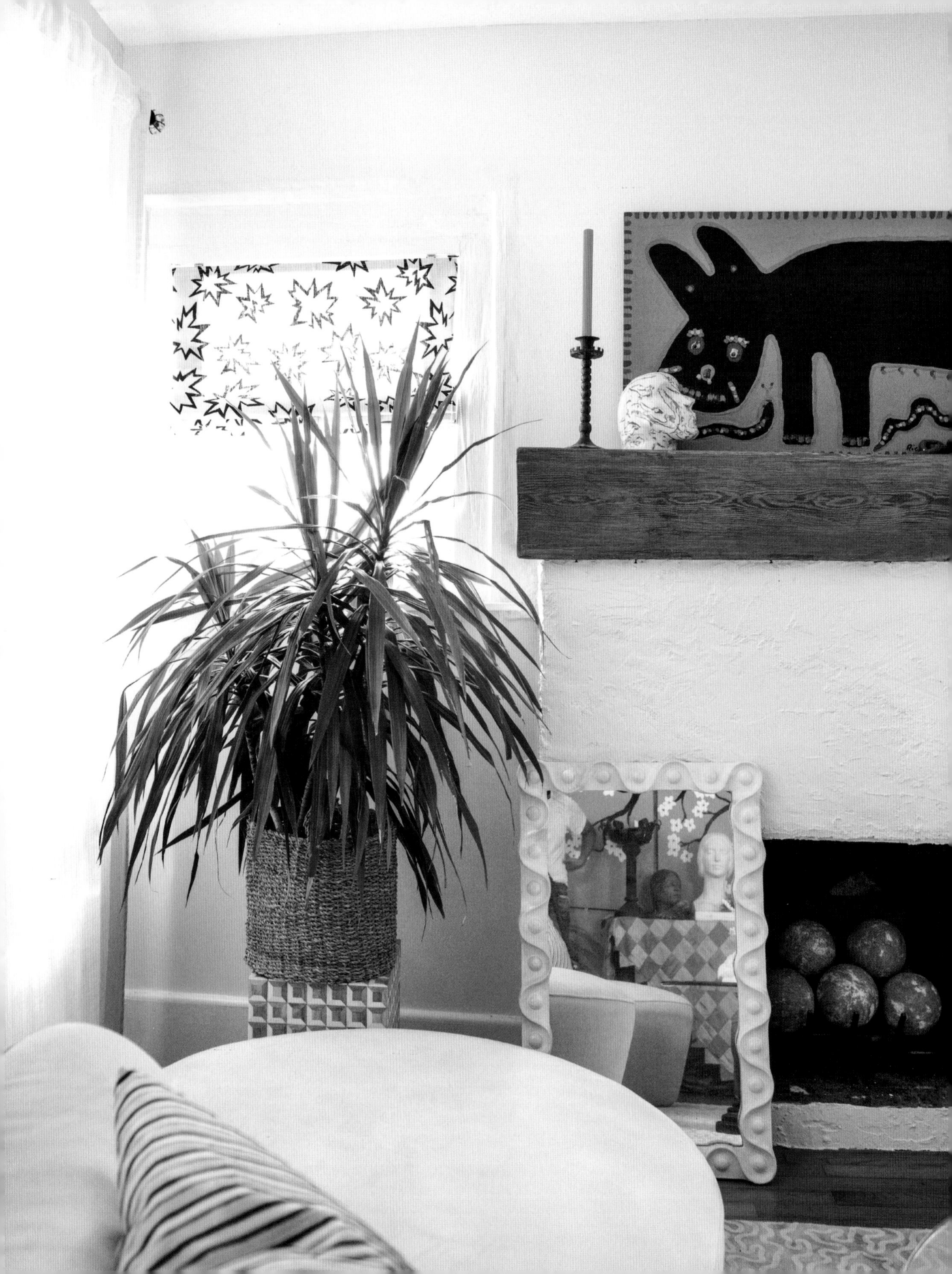

Basic Formula of Room Design

I USE A VERY SIMPLE FORMULA when approaching the design of a room. Whenever you feel overwhelmed by a space, just return to this:

Groundwork + Layout + Accessories = Finished Room

GROUNDWORK

By groundwork, I mean starting from the bottom up: Determine if you plan on changing out the flooring or using rugs. I am very pro rug, as they instantly make a space feel warm and provide added visual interest. They, quite literally, ground a space and can carve out smaller niches in large rooms (for instance, placing a rug in the corner with a desk subtly demarcates an "office" nook). I use rugs beneath dining tables, beds, and coffee tables and will even layer them on top of one another to create a clash of patterns. Laying this groundwork will naturally lead you to the best layout of the room.

LAYOUT

Next, move on to how you'd like everything to be arranged. The layout should include both the larger pieces of furniture (couches, beds, tables, and desks) as well as the static elements of the home itself (windows, doors, built-ins). This is a good time to take measurements of what you already have for the room and sketch out a simple floor plan to get an idea of what else you'll need and where things will go.

Determine your focal point. Perhaps the focal point of the room is a TV, in which case you should decide if you want to hang it on the wall or need some sort of stand, and then build the room out from there. Or maybe the room has a wonderful fireplace or a huge, bare wall that's begging for an interesting piece of artwork. Ask yourself what you want people to notice first when they walk into the room, and then create your layout around that.

Similarly, anticipate how the space will be used and ensure that it feels livable. Rather than sticking a single chair in a corner, place it next to a side table or floor lamp, so it can become a cozy reading spot, or, better yet, near the sofa, so it can be used as extra seating when you have company.

ACCESSORIES

Now that you have the overall room arrangement pinned down, you can start to layer in the pieces that tell your story: the art! the trinkets! the blankets and throws! This final step is what will make your home feel personalized. When hunting for accessories, be sure to consider small pieces of furniture, such as stools, ottomans, and poufs. Not only do these take up space in a room and make it feel much cozier, but they're also easy to rearrange and multifunctional—and can become handy seats for any last-minute guests at holiday gatherings.

ABOVE **This naked lady (from an antiques mall) has lived in nearly every room of my house.**

My grandmother, having been born and
raised in the part of the country that
birthed a number of the greats, was an
avid collector of Southern folk art. I like
the high-impact visual of displaying all
of her beloved art dolls together like
one little family and adore the juxtaposition of styling them with a very
1990s set of lithographs atop a piece of
clean-lined furniture.

Tell Your Story

THE MOST INTERESTING INTERIORS are those in which you get a strong sense of someone's interests, their passions, and all the fun quirks that make them unique. The basics of room design serve to make you feel comfortable, but the aesthetic makes it feel like you. Now that we have the basics down, let's get to the fun part: layering and accessorizing to make your home your own.

COLLECT THEM ALL

Sometimes one of something is ugly or random, but a bunch of those same "somethings" is really cool. I once saw a beautiful photo of Martha Stewart's jadeite collection and was taken aback at how incredibly modern the pieces looked when displayed together. Jadeite, a type of green glass popularized in the 1940s and '50s, tends to look very retro. Of course, in Martha's hands—and lining the wooden cabinets and shelves of her Maine estate—the material looks modern and even artful.

Keep the following in mind when displaying a collection:

→ Displaying a large group of items in one unifying color will create cohesion (and look a lot less cluttered).
→ Curate your collection so that the best pieces are displayed most prominently.
→ Set aside one key area (like a bookshelf, a cabinet, or along a console table) for a collection. This will make it look much more intentional than placing items throughout a space.

DO MORE WITH LESS

Minimalism can be challenging (IMO, even more so than maximalism), because every piece is working overtime. With fewer items, everything is a tad more naked, so every bit and bauble really needs to look its best. Here are a few tips for brightening up a minimal interior.

Decorate with plants: A little greenery goes a long way and makes a minimalist space feel more thoughtful and lived in.

Think tonally: Minimal doesn't necessarily mean all white. Add depth by layering shades of neutrals.

Consider texture: To ensure a minimalist space doesn't feel too cold or stark, incorporate lots of textures with a variety of neutral fabrics and materials.

Make a statement: If your space is cool, calm, and collected, you can still inject some personality with an interesting piece of art or a well-designed accessory. If you're going for neutral, look for art that's sculptural—curved is, of course, sexy, and especially so in a room that's begging for extra oomph.

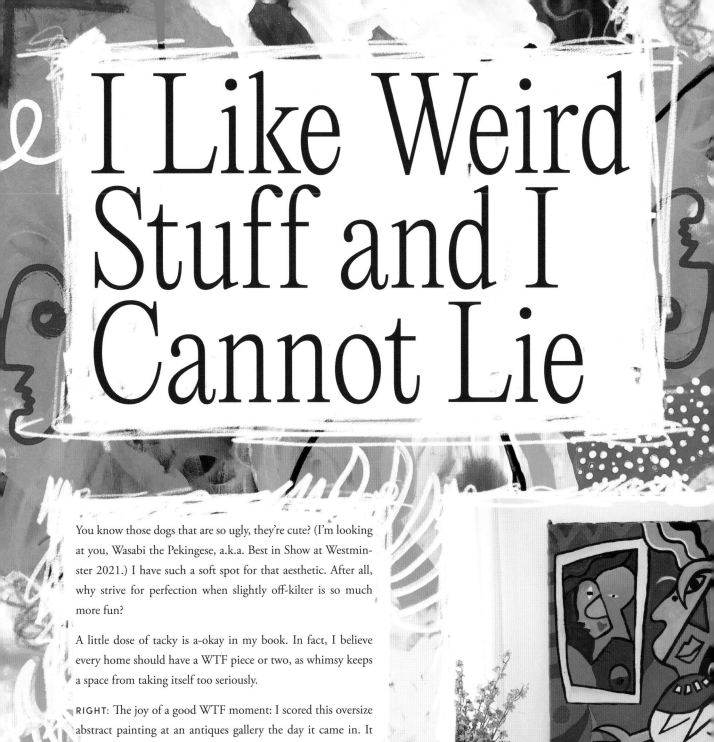

I Like Weird Stuff and I Cannot Lie

You know those dogs that are so ugly, they're cute? (I'm looking at you, Wasabi the Pekingese, a.k.a. Best in Show at Westminster 2021.) I have such a soft spot for that aesthetic. After all, why strive for perfection when slightly off-kilter is so much more fun?

A little dose of tacky is a-okay in my book. In fact, I believe every home should have a WTF piece or two, as whimsy keeps a space from taking itself too seriously.

RIGHT: The joy of a good WTF moment: I scored this oversize abstract painting at an antiques gallery the day it came in. It was painted by a retired art teacher and used to teach children about Picasso. It's no Picasso itself, of course, but I love the story, the colors, the patterns, and the scale.

OR DO THE MOST

I am a maximalist through and through. I know it can be tempting to go HAM when it comes to maximalism, throwing anything and everything on the walls and furniture. But maximal doesn't equate to hot mess. In a room full of stuff, the stuff should still look considered. Below are some tips to help you make a maximalist space look sophisticated rather than sloppy.

Choose a theme: Creating a theme can bring unity to a room. Create a vision of who might live in the space—an old sailor, perhaps, or a British heiress who decamped to Beverly Hills in the late '90s—and decorate based on that singular idea.

Keep it in the family: While you don't necessarily need to stick to one single color in a maximalist room, it's a good idea to pair like colors: like orange with pink or green with blue. This creates cohesion but still offers that layered look.

Make it yours: Most important, design wholeheartedly. Even if it doesn't hit all the criteria of a well-designed space (symmetry, complementary colors), it can still be great as long as you love it. If all else fails, just allow something to grow on you. Sometimes the longer you stare at something, the more intentional it seems.

OPPOSITE: There's beauty in the overstuffed, in the glorious and (maybe just slightly) garish. The fun in designing a maximalist space is that rules need not apply. The point is not to match. Spare white walls and distressed wood bowls are serene, but random objects, layers of texture and pattern, and an ever-growing collection of artistic ephemera? Now that's just sexy. In my living room, an ever-rotating collection of colorful art hangs out with an overstuffed sofa, designer leather bench (used as a coffee table), and lots of patterned smalls.

OPPOSITE **This gallery
wall is home to art-
work spanning from
the early 1900s to
the early 2000s.**

MIX AND MATCH

We talked about design styles at the beginning of this book. There are so many, all wildly different, but in the 2020s, you don't have to stick with one aesthetic like Mid-Century or Art Deco. What might seem diametrically opposed on paper can actually blend together quite seamlessly in person. In fact, blending items from various time periods tends to look less "retro" than outfitting a room in one singular era. Balancing a very traditional mahogany dining table with a Mid-Mod chrome pendant light, for instance, feels fresh and unexpected, inciting a visual game of push and pull.

ABOVE: I went into overdrive with the mixies and matchies here, pairing a coral-patterned velvet headboard from the 1990s with a 1950s folk-art-style painting.

Vintage Jargon 101

HERE'S SOME INSIDER LINGO. FAMILIARIZE YOURSELF SO YOU CAN SOUND LIKE A PRO:

ANTIQUE: Technically speaking, anything more than 100 years old (though "vintage" and "antique" are often used interchangeably)

BUNDLE: A group of items purchased in bulk, for a lower price

FCFS: First come, first served (a phrase you'll see a lot on Facebook Marketplace; in short, it means no holds)

FIRM: A nonnegotiable price

NFS: The three worst words in the English language: Not. For. Sale

NWT/NWOT: New with tags/new without tags

OBO: Or best offer

PPU: Pending pickup

PRE-VINTAGE: Not old enough to be "vintage," technically, but still kinda old (10–15 years)

SMALLS: Tiny items (knickknacks, trinkets), also sometimes known as "walkouts"

TURN: An item that has some opportunity for profit built into the margins (a piece you buy and resell)

VINTAGE: Generally, a piece between 30 and 100 years old

WHAT'S THE DEATH ON THIS?: What's the lowest a dealer will go on a particular item?

Living Large

THERE ARE A FEW EASY WAYS to make any space feel larger than it actually is. Here are my favorite secrets.

HANG CURTAINS HIGH

I once read in *Architectural Digest* that curtains should be hung 4 to 6 inches above the window frame, and I've never looked back. When the curtains are higher than the window itself, it makes the window look so. Much. Bigger. This trick also works for furniture and built-ins. If you can, bring bookcases and cabinets all the way to the ceiling. Everyone's eyes will travel up as a result, creating the appearance of a sky-high space.

Got a lot of art? It, too, can expand all the way to the ceiling (this is an especially stunning visual for a gallery wall). A well-placed mirror can also work wonders, casting light up and outward, and making the room feel more spacious.

PULL YOUR FURNITURE AWAY FROM THE WALL

Everyone always wants to stick their couch right up against the wall, thinking it frees up space in the center of the room. In reality—and counterintuitively—it makes the room look smaller and blocks the sunlight if your couch sits in front of a window. I'm begging you: Pull your couch, chairs, and end tables several feet (or at least inches) out from the wall. It makes the room more livable, too, as it doesn't require you to scream at someone seated in the chair opposite.

When Bigger is Better

A CASE FOR OVERSIZE ART

When it comes to art, I'm definitely in the "Go big or go home" camp. I love a gallery wall (more on that on page 139), but sometimes, all you need is one big, chunky piece of goodness to make a statement.

However, don't buy a piece just because it's oversize. As with any art in your home, look for work that moves you, makes you happy, and won't bore you—or irritate you—after a couple of weeks.

Don't be scared to let a painting or oversize poster dominate your space. (You will, of course, want to measure your wall first, to ensure the piece won't be too big.) That's kind of the point with oversize art. Or you can create an impactful color story by opting for a large-scale painting that complements other bold pieces in a room.

In addition to scale, keep in mind proportion: how the piece in question relates to other pieces in the same room. Diversify the size of art, playing with the balance of big and small. Similar to how you might place two chairs opposite one sofa, you can pair one large painting with two smaller works.

OPPOSITE: In my living room, two large-scale works of art flank a window for maximum impact. The pink piece on the left was made by me—proof that if you can't find exactly what you want, you can always just make it yourself. (Thrift stores are full of large canvases that can easily be painted over and are typically much more affordable than a new canvas at a craft store.)

PLACE TABLES WITHIN REACH OF SEATING

Placing a coffee table roughly 20 inches from a sofa ensures you can easily access your morning latte (or takeout, if you're like me and think things taste better when eaten on the couch). Similarly, keep side tables within a foot of a couch or bed, and keep them at similar heights so you don't hit your elbow on the table when reaching for a cup of water late at night.

DISPLAY ART AT EYE LEVEL

There's a reason art galleries and museums hang art at eye level. It's easier for the viewer (or homeowner) to appreciate the work. (Too high, and your neck aches from staring up; too low, and the room feels much shorter, because you've created a cutoff point at the top of the frame.) Art hung at eye level also creates a flow, allowing the eye to move around the room with ease. The pros advise that the center of a piece of art be anywhere from 57 to 60 inches from the floor. If it's going above a piece of furniture—a chair, a table, a couch—aim to hang the art 4 to 6 inches above.

LAYER YOUR LIGHTS

Adding layers of light—via chandeliers, table lamps, and accent lights—creates glow and shadow. It also adds dimension to a space and feels more purposeful. Your overhead light illuminates the entire room, while smaller fixtures help accent accessories and create a warm ambience.

Styling Tricks

WHILE I AM NOT A TRAINED INTERIOR DESIGNER, I have picked up a handful of ways to make a space feel much more pulled together and thought out—all the better for showcasing your amazing finds.

DESIGNATE A GALLERY WALL

The gallery wall has evolved over time, and I think it's safe to say it has surpassed "trend" status. Layering makes any space feel instantly cooler, and your walls are a prime example: Stack, layer, and showcase pretty pieces by keeping the following in mind.

→ The art on a gallery wall needn't be comprised of only one subject—I think it's actually more fun if you mix, say, abstract pieces with traditional ones—but there should be some unity. This might mean sticking to similar color palettes or using similarly colored frames. It's all about making a statement without making a mess.

→ Gallery walls can coexist with shelves or tables, and don't be afraid to arrange art around a doorframe. Anywhere there's wall space, art can be, too.

→ Go beyond square paintings, adding interest with other small pieces that can be hung, such as mirrors, sconces, and even decorative plates. A wall of art is so much more special when there's a variety of shapes on it.

OPPOSITE: I may have extolled the benefits of large-scale art previously, but size isn't everything; sometimes it really is all about how you use it. This is the case with super-small works of art, which can have their own impact. On my dining room wall, I mixed in a few diminutive mirrors and portraits with the other, standard-sized stuff. The placement and size of the smaller works makes for its own sort of statement.

DECK OUT THE MANTLE

Many of us turn to our fireplaces come holiday season, adorning them with a strand of garland or maybe a row of nutcrackers that we'll glance at until January, stow away, and then do it all again the next year. But mantles are focal points in a room already, so it makes sense to have them looking fresh and interesting all year round.

Here are my tried-and-true tips for topping a mantle.

→ When creating a vignette atop your mantle, try to mix heights (something tall with something short) and finishes (something shiny with something dull).

→ Stick with asymmetry. Odd groupings of items—whether we're talking art or accessories—create interest and allow your eye to bounce around. Playing with proportions is really fun and very sophisticated if done well. It's the reason Jenna Lyons's outfits always look so good: She mixes short with long, tailored with relaxed, and voluminous with sleek. Think of your mantle in the same way you might build an outfit (or, at least, the way Jenna might).

→ By that same token, use odd numbers of decorative items so the finished product has interesting proportions. If you have four candlesticks, take one away; up the ante by placing two on one side of the mantle and the remaining one on the other side. Remember: Slightly off-kilter is a bit more chic.

OPPOSITE: My fireplace used to drive me crazy. It was white when I bought my house, and one day, in a fit of boredom, I mixed concrete in my living room and applied it by hand to the entire thing, for a more plastered look. I don't necessarily recommend doing that, but it's a good lesson in how small changes can equate to a major transformation. On top of the mantle, I leaned a folk-art painting by the late artist Richard Burnside in the center, flanked by multicolored candles in iron candlesticks. For further interest, I added an upside-down candle mold (it looks pretty sculptural, so why not?), a vintage chain, and a marbled sculpture of a head.

GET CREATIVE WITH THE CONSOLE

Don't be overwhelmed by the endless possibilities that come with styling a console or sofa table. Keep the following in mind, and topping your table will be a cinch.

→ The word to keep in mind when it comes to console styling is weight. Hefty pieces—lamps, oversize sculptures, weird wooden cats like the one in this photo—are a great place to start.

→ Next, add more diminutive things until you land at the sweet spot, which is really just whatever makes you happy. Stacking books underneath a piece of decor can bring height as well as an interesting dimension to the finished look.

→ If you have the space, create a gallery wall over and around the entire table. I did this in my dining room, even though it runs counterintuitive to every design rule ever (which would require that you hang art first, decorate a table second).

→ Not into a gallery wall or want one big impact? Incorporate your art into the console itself: Lean a mirror against the wall on top of the table, or hang a single piece of artwork, centered over the top, with accessories placed in front of it.

RETHINK TEXTILES

You can use textiles to create an altogether different piece of furniture. Drape a sheepskin rug over a low sofa, and it looks like it's been reupholstered. A vintage tablecloth or quilt tossed over a boring console does the same, adding a dose of punch and pattern to a room in the process. And perhaps one of my favorite outside-the-box styling tricks is to drape a jacket over a low or child-size stool. The result is a draped, artful side table that everyone will ask about.

The one seen here is just an adjustable stool, positioned as low as it can go and covered with a sequined jacket.

Textiles can also double as art. If you're dying for a piece of oversize art, one great place to look is the floor. Estate sales almost always offer vintage rugs, and many are in pristine condition.

TIP! If you're looking to hang a small rug or textile (3' x 5' or under) on the wall, try encasing it in a floating acrylic frame, which will add visual weight without taking away from the pattern or texture.

LAYER LIKE A BOSS

It actually takes a lot of effort to convey that lived-in-but-sophisticated, oh-this-old-thing? look, though most designers won't tell you that. Layering can be especially tough to pull off. While there are no hard-and-fast rules for layering a space, here are a few guidelines that might help.

Add in some old stuff: Vintage and antique pieces convey a sense of soul that nothing else can match. Even if you have new furniture from a big-name chain, a handful of smaller vintage accessories (an old globe, a weathered terra-cotta sculpture) can provide a room with so much character.

Use rugs: Try carpeting a large space with an oversize rug (something neutral like jute) and layering a small throw rug over top. This helps lend intimacy and comfort to a room.

Don't forget your lights: I've already touched on the importance of lighting, but it's well worth revisiting. Light is not only a way to glow-up your space, but it can also be layered. Aim for an assortment of heights, including ceiling, wall, and table-level fixtures.

MIX PATTERNS LIKE A PRO

Most of us are taught about the horrors of "clashing" from an early age, as we first begin to dress ourselves. But pairing pattern on pattern can be fun—and even sophisticated—when done well. Here's how.

Treat certain prints as neutrals: Prints containing neutral colors (like black-and-white checkerboard or brown-on-black leopard) can ground a space and pair with nearly any other pattern.

Aim for relatable patterns: If you're going for a range of prints in a space, try to anchor them with a common theme (like a similar color palette or motif).

…But add contrast, too: A contrasting color or pattern can really strike a fun balance in a room. Don't overwhelm: Add in some solid colors to break up all the patterns and help a space feel less haphazard.

Vary the scale: Stick to one pattern that is overscale (a large print on a small stool, for instance), and vary the scale on all the other patterns in a space.

Find your base: To ensure a space looks deliberate, think about one material or color or pattern that can serve as your base in the room. In my bedroom, for instance, I played with plenty of patterns but kept them in small doses (a floral on the bed, black and white on the accessories). My base is really a light gold hue, which is seen on the laminate burl side tables and oversize gold mirror. Utilizing one throughline and layering in punchy patterns over that creates a more well-rounded aesthetic.

The Art of the Upgrade

WHILE UPCYCLING MIGHT CALL TO MIND a mason jar candleholder, there are plenty of other modern ways to make over your vintage finds. Here are some of my favorite go-to ideas for making something old new again.

PROFESSIONAL REUPHOLSTERING

OK, so I'm not going to provide you with a step-by-step of reupholstering, and for good reason: It's best left to the professionals. This is particularly true because I gravitate to really interesting (complicated) shapes of furniture that I would destroy if I attempted to re-cover with a staple gun and some fancy fabric. Reupholstering is pricey, no doubt about it—anywhere from $400 to $1,000 for a chair, including the cost of the fabric—but it's worth it if you bought the chair for, say, $10. Keep in mind that very well-loved upholstered furniture may require extra attention (and more money), as the stuffing and springs could need replacing.

PAINTED PAGE FROM A VINTAGE BOOK

This is so easy, it doesn't require a step-by-step. I love buying vintage art books at thrift stores, tearing out a page, and adding a splash of paint. This is especially fun to do on a page that includes a portrait (use a bit of paint to cover the eyes, for instance), but you can also create your own portrait by painting a funny face on a page full of text. Pop it in a vintage frame and you'll have your own one-of-a-kind work of art.

ABOVE **Scour the thrift store for vintage frames.**

WALLPAPERED LAMPSHADE

A simple lampshade makes for an easy DIY project. First, measure that bad boy, then cut your wallpaper or fabric to the shade's height and one inch wider than its circumference. Brush a thin layer of white craft glue and water (a two-to-one mix) on the ugly side of the paper or fabric. Press it onto the shade, leaving a half inch of fabric or wallpaper at the top and bottom. Fold the excess paper or fabric over the edges of the shade (using double-sided tape can provide extra hold), and work out any wrinkles as you go.

ABOVE **Think outside the box and use a quilt (or a blanket) as a tablecloth.**

MAKE IT A TABLE

Another outside-the-box design trick is to create tables with trunks or benches. My Goyard trunk is so oversize that I style it in the corner of a room, typically with a lamp or stack of books on top. In my living room, I've also employed this trick, using a thrifted leather Mitchell Gold + Bob Williams bench (scored for $50) as a coffee table. A bench also works at the foot of the bed, to make the bed appear longer and serve as an easy place to toss your throw pillows before you go to bed.

ODD KNUTSEN

GOYARD TRUNK

NO-NAME ART

HAND CHAIRS

BRASS

TOGO

VLADIMIR KAGAN

My All-Time Favorite Finds

THOUGH MY GOAL IS OFTEN TO FLIP MY FINDS (or, at least, live with them until I crave something new), there are a handful of pieces that I will treasure forever. Here are a few of my personal favorite thrift, vintage, and antique finds, and the stories behind them.

GOYARD TRUNK

Purchased for: $90
Value: $10,000+

Several years ago, my grandmother and I were stuck in traffic after leaving an estate sale when we saw a sign that read "Old wicker." Naturally, we pulled over to browse while we waited out rush hour.

The store itself was fine, but we didn't find much. We were on our way out when the elderly woman who owned the shop said, "Be sure to check out the shed out back before you leave."

That's where we saw it: A 4-foot Goyard trunk that opens to include a row of drawers and places to store jewelry and small accessories. I screamed when I rounded the corner and saw it and then screamed even harder when I read the price tag: "Old trunk, $90."

The owner said someone had found it in their attic and brought it to the shop. Apparently, neither one had any idea what they had on their hands. I shoved that baby in my trunk faster than you can google "Goyard," paid, and was on my way.

1970S MASTERCRAFT BRASS CHAIRS

Purchased for: $100
Value: $2,500+

I found this set of six Mastercraft brass dining chairs in a Salvation Army outside Orlando, Florida. It was probably one of my best thrift-store experiences, as the same store also had an oversize brutalist chest by Lane and a stunning console table. But with only my SUV and still a few hours away from home, it was like having to pick only queso, salsa, or guac. The chairs were so unique that I opted for them and left the other items at the store for another lucky shopper.

ODD KNUTSEN LUNA CHAIRS

Purchased for: $50
Value: $4,000

These Craigslist finds came from a home where they were rarely used, so the chairs were in excellent condition. The iconic, low-back Scandinavian design makes for a wildly comfortable seat, and they have that laid-back look that could read masculine or feminine, depending on your aesthetic.

HAND-SHAPED CHAIRS

Purchased for: $5 and $25
Value: $500+

I can't say no to a body part, and hands, especially, speak to me. I purchased both of these hand chairs on Facebook Marketplace, from two different owners. They aren't really "by" anyone, and I think Walmart actually mass-produced these years ago. But that doesn't matter to me. The point is, they are unique, a statement piece, and rare. Some items mass-produced by chain stores are no longer being made, making them collectible in their own right. (In fact, I sold one for over $500.)

VLADIMIR KAGAN NAUTILUS CHAIRS

Purchased for: $100
Value: $3,000+

Obviously, I had to jump when I saw these chairs on Facebook Marketplace, but I got a little nervous when the seller didn't want to share their address until minutes before I arrived. It turns out, they belonged to a professional athlete (hence the hesitancy to disclose where he lived) and had previously decorated his bachelor pad. I love these chairs, because they can go in so many directions, depending on how you style them: With Lucite light fixtures, they are pure Hollywood Regency, but pair them with some leather and chrome, and you can really dial down the one-night-stand factor.

TOGO SOFA

Purchased for: $40
Value: $2,000+

I found this sofa after a full day of thrifting in central Florida. I went to at least 20 stores that day and decided, on my way home, to pop into just one more. This was waiting for me. I pulled the tag (which read, "Gaming chair") in dramatic fashion and stuffed it in my car, thrilled with my spoils. Yes, it was a stellar find, but it was also a good lesson in the importance of tenacity. Just because you walk in one store (or 10) that doesn't appear to have much, you might still find something special elsewhere. Take it from me and adhere to your ABTs: Always. Be. Thrifting.

NO-NAME ART

Purchased for: $5+
Value: ???

I've found some valuable pieces of art, but none really compare, at least visually, to a fun abstract piece created by an outsider artist. Many of the pieces in my home were thrift finds, and I love each one more than the last; none are by any "listed" artists, but that doesn't matter to me. They have that made-by-hand feeling you can't find at a chain store. In general, abstract art is great, because it adds such a fun punch of color and can take on so many different meanings.

PART FOUR

HOW TO SELL

I NEVER REALLY SET OUT TO BE AN ANTIQUES DEALER. Instead, it came about naturally: As a collector, I eventually had items I needed to off-load, and so will you.

Over the years, I've sold antique clothing, furniture, art, and accessories on Etsy, eBay, Chairish, Facebook Marketplace, Craigslist, and Instagram, at yard sales—occasionally hosted by me—and in a gallery.

What have I learned? You can make pretty good money "turning tables," as I call it (that is, flipping vintage stuff). But as with most small businesses, you'll also be investing a lot of yourself and your cold, hard cash. So don't start a vintage business with the express purpose of making money. Do it because you love it, and all that other stuff will follow.

Clichéd? Maybe. But trust me when I say you really have to love something to be willing to rent a cargo van, drive it across state lines, walk into a total stranger's house, and lift a 100-pound couch over your head before schlepping it all the way back home.

Here's what to know about selling vintage.

The Investment

OF COURSE, TO SELL VINTAGE YOU HAVE TO BUY VINTAGE. But there is so much more you'll be investing in when you launch a resale biz, including your time—unquestionably the most valuable resource of all.

PRODUCT

You'll want to set a budget for how much you're willing to spend on inventory and keep track of your receipts as you go. (This can be difficult at estate sales, which often handwrite receipts or don't provide any at all. Do your best.) The common rule in retail is to mark things up at double what you paid for them wholesale. With vintage, there is no written rule: I've found things for $11 and sold them for $600, but I've also found things for $20 and sold them for $30.

Before you begin scrolling through Facebook Marketplace for items, nail down how much you're comfortable spending for an entire month's worth of inventory.

MANPOWER

Here's the thing about vintage furniture: That ish is heavy. Add to that the fact that most thrift stores are run by volunteers and don't always have a team to help you load an item into your car, and you can expect to do a lot of heavy lifting. If you don't want to throw your back out for a $25 table, though, you can call in a delivery guy. That will cost money, of course, so a $25 table might end up costing you $125 when all is said and done.

STORAGE

Trinkets and paintings don't seem like they take up a lot of space—until you have 500 of them. Renting a storage unit is a great idea if you want to store your inventory in a safe space with enough room to breathe (rather than piling it in a corner of your garage). Some sellers even use their storage space as a showroom of sorts, styling the items so a potential buyer can come have a look and see what it might look like in their own home.

SHIPPING SUPPLIES

Shipping is, without a doubt, the most annoyingly difficult part of vintage selling. I love Amazon Prime as much as anybody, but it's really spoiled us all into believing that anything can be shipped fast and for free. In reality, shipping costs can run into the thousands for a large painting, and even then, there's no guarantee it won't be destroyed in transit. I always keep shipping in mind when buying anything. Large pieces of furniture sent cross-country require white-glove shipping, so research the companies that provide it. (There are also some Uber-like start-ups that are slightly less expensive.) Even small items, such as ceramic plates, will require boxes, packing peanuts, bubble wrap, and tape. If you know of a local store that throws out boxes and peanuts, see if they might work out a deal to provide them to you, which is far less wasteful. As far as tape goes, invest in the good stuff. I am not #sponsored by Gorilla Tape, but let me tell you, that stuff holds my entire life together and is far superior to the other tape products on the market. (That's the kind of X-rated stuff you'll talk about if you start selling vintage.)

MARKETING

While the use of some sites—Facebook Marketplace, Craigslist—is free, others can cost (a lot of) money. Some, such as Chairish, even allow you to pay a monthly fee to market your finds on the site, which could yield more sales, considering more people see the items. Social media can come in extremely handy, too—more on this later—but can also add up financially if you pay for promoted posts often enough.

Other Basics

THE LOOK

Rather than buying anything that seems remotely cool and sellable, settle on an aesthetic—Mid-Century masculine, Palm Beach funky—and try to ensure that everything you sell falls into that category (just like my grandmother and her Shabby Chic). That doesn't mean you only have to sell one particular item or decade, but it should all fit seamlessly together. A good way to define your style as a seller is to look at the pieces in your own home—the stuff you gravitate to already—and determine what ties it all together. The items I sell all tend to be hypercolorful, abstract, and sculptural pieces that look like they fit in the same home. And that's because I keep buying for the same person: Me.

You can also get even more specific, homing in on items made in one particular moment in time or by one brand. Even some rare, out-of-production IKEA pieces have become highly collectible in recent years. If that's your bag, go all in, learning everything you can about the brand, its past collections, and its collaborations and heading to the shops with that in mind.

Before you start selling, determine what you love and who you want to buy for, and carve out your niche. Over time, you'll become a resource for whatever look or brand you focus on, and your curated aesthetic will set you apart from the millions of other vintage sellers already out there.

SOURCING

Obviously, I love a thrift store for sourcing vintage. They have such a high turnover of merchandise, and the prices really can't be beat. But they are not easy to shop, and you can feel very defeated if you don't find anything.

There's really no secret formula for finding great vintage in a thrift store, other than having a ton of tenacity. If you start to feel discouraged, take a day trip to a less populated city or an area where the stores are less picked over than your usual spots.

Perhaps the greatest thing about vintage is that the supply will never run out. There's plenty of stuff out there, waiting to be scooped up, even if you don't find it today.

LEARNING TO LIVE WITH IT

A wise man once said, "Don't get high on your own supply," but it's advice that I don't always heed when it comes to vintage finds. Buying what you love (even if you're just going to sell it later) makes the process so much more fun. I am passionate about the vintage I buy and get really excited when I see a piece that's very "me," because I know it will also resonate with those who gravitate to my particular aesthetic. And if it doesn't sell, then I'm the one who scores.

PRICING YOUR PRODUCT

The more established you are as a vintage seller, the easier it will be to find a home for a $1,000 coffee table or $500 piece of art. Until then, you'll need to price to sell—but not too low, as that could make it difficult to turn a profit.

Just as you would when hunting for vintage, you'll need to do research to settle on a sweet spot, pricewise. I always take into account not just how other sellers priced an item, but also what I paid. For instance, if I bought a table for $20, and it's being sold on 1stDibs for $2,000, I'm more than happy to price it on the lower end of the spectrum.

Over time, you'll get an idea of what's fair versus what is completely outrageous, but when you're just starting out, keep the following in mind: purchase cost, availability, quality, and trendiness. As a general rule, if you buy it for one, you sell it for two, so you should start by doubling the price you paid for an item. But also do your research: Is the same (or a similar) item available elsewhere, by another seller? By many sellers? If so, it's widely available and not a rare find. Do a price comparison and ensure your item is at least in the same ballpark. Lastly, if you have nothing to compare it to, think about how trendy it is. Maybe it's a no-name work of art, but it's something that an interior designer would go nuts over. Price accordingly.

Where to Sell

IN TODAY'S WORLD, THERE ARE DOZENS OF VENUES where you can sell vintage, from in person to online. Here are a few of the best options.

ONLINE RESALE MARKETPLACE

Best for: Quickly off-loading things you no longer use and can't sell elsewhere
What to know: There are people who literally make a career out of flipping furniture on Facebook Marketplace, but it's also a great option when you just need to get rid of large items fast. Depending on what you purchased the piece for, you could turn a profit, but prices on sites such as Craigslist, OfferUp, and Facebook Marketplace tend to be low and competitive. I use these most often for selling an item I'm about to replace, and I always specify "No delivery" or "Need help to transport" if it's an especially heavy item.

YARD SALE

Best for: Freeing up space in your garage or storage unit
What to know: You're probably not going to turn a profit at a yard sale, and that's not really the point. I host yard sales when I have way too much stuff in my house/garage/storage and quickly need to free up space (like when I have a lot of items that have gone unsold). Yard sales are best for racks of clothes and smalls. I wouldn't recommend them for off-loading heavy pieces of furniture, as most casual yard sale shoppers won't have the space or manpower to lift and tote home an oversize armoire, media unit, or sofa.

SOCIAL MEDIA

Best for: Casting a wide net to share your newest finds
What to know: I tend to share my most recent vintage finds once a week on Instagram (#thriftscorethursday, holler if you hear me), which is a great way to forge a connection with other vintage fiends like me and also turn over items quickly.

Pricewise, I'd compare Instagram sales to in-person yard sales or online market-places. You might not bring in a huge profit, but for me, it's more about meeting like-minded thrifters and sharing the stories behind some of your favorite finds.

Also of note: Social media allows you to gauge an immediate reaction to your finds or your eye for styling, in real time. You can literally see, based on likes and comments, how much an item resonates with people (so if you see something similar in the future, you'll know it's a worthy buy).

BOOTH AT AN ANTIQUES GALLERY

Best for: Those who love to style
What to know: An antiques gallery is never going to reach the same audience as you would online, since you're really only able to sell to those who physically shop inside the store. That being said, those shopping in an antiques gallery are generally looking for great old stuff, are willing to pay a higher price to get it, and appreciate good styling. And that is truly the biggest upside of selling in a gallery: having an entire room to play in, creating vignettes and styling items so that customers can get inspiration and a sense of what a piece might look like if they bring it home. (I've even heard tales of some dealers styling their booths so well that customers buy the entire lot of merchandise outright.)

CONSIGNMENT SHOP

Best for: Selling a few pieces of furniture because you have zero space for it at home
What to know: Consignment stores are great for those who aren't necessarily inter-ested in starting a vintage-selling business but do have some higher-quality pieces that they need to rehome. A consignment store will take a cut but they'll deal with the sale, the delivery, and the storage of the piece until it attracts a buyer.

POP-UP MARKETS

Best for: Newbie sellers who crave that human connection
What to know: In-person, pop-up vintage markets allow new sellers to meet like-minded buyers as well as local vendors who've been in the game for a while. But most buyers are looking for less-expensive, easy-to-carry items, so mix a lot of smalls (or even racks of clothing, if that's your jam) in with a couple of higher-ticket items.

VIRTUAL VINTAGE SITE

Best for: Those who have the time, energy, and space to devote to a vintage-flipping side gig

What to know: The beauty of sites such as Etsy, Chairish, and 1stDibs is that they are already set up, are user friendly, and have a built-in customer base. You just can't compete with that reach, even if you have amazing SEO skills.

There are downsides, of course. Some of these sites take a portion of your proceeds, and some charge a fee just to list an item. But the fees are nominal, and you won't have to worry about the overhead of building your own website or opening your own brick-and-mortar shop.

Also of note: To make selling vintage online a worthwhile endeavor (the kind you could quit your day job for) will require a considerable amount of time and energy, not to mention financial resources. If you are interested in selling dozens of items via one of these sites, you will benefit from growing a base of followers (which, trust me, takes years) and constantly replenishing your merchandise. No one likes going into a store and seeing the same items every time.

You will also have to worry about buying shipping supplies, packing the items yourself (or paying a shipping service to do it), delivery, storage, insurance, keeping track of receipts for tax purposes … you get the picture. It's absolutely doable to turn a profit selling vintage online, but, as with any business, it requires hard work.

Conclusion

AS WE'VE LEARNED IN RECENT YEARS, our homes are our sanctuaries—and often our workspaces, our gyms, our places to eat takeout and binge Netflix dating shows until we go cross-eyed. Design might have been considered frivolous for decades, but now it's an important way to make our spaces feel, well, more like us.

One of my design pillars is that you can have a very polished space filled with high-quality yet incredibly affordable pieces. But that requires a) finding the items, b) styling them, and c) eventually figuring out what to do with them if you ever move or redecorate. I hope I detailed all of the above here, offering you tips for hunting down the pieces to transform your space, tricks for putting them together with what you already have, and a couple of options for how to get rid of them once you're bored.

Of course, if you aren't interested in selling your castoffs, there's always my favorite option: donating. I bet there's someone, somewhere, who would be more than willing to breathe new energy into your old things.

Resources

IDENTIFICATION

ANTIQUE MARKS | *antique-marks.com*
More than 10,000 antique marks for pottery, porcelain, china, and more, with high-quality images as examples

CONNECTED LINES FURNITURE STYLE GUIDE | *connectedlines.com/styleguide*
A guide for identifying antique and vintage furniture styles, with illustrations and identifying markers to help you determine in what era a piece was made

KOVELS ANTIQUES INC. | *kovels.com*
A consistently updated site full of everything from pricing info and forums to a very cool "Collector's Questions" page, where collectors share images and the backstory of a particular item, and the site's professionals respond with more info about the maker and the possible value—kind of like a virtual *Antiques Roadshow*

REAL OR REPRO | *realorrepro.com*
A source for identifying fake or copied versions of antique items

TRADEMARKIA | *trademarkia.com*
A search engine that helps you identify vintage items and the date they were produced

PRICING

ANTIQUES ROADSHOW APPRAISALS ARCHIVE | *pbs.org/wgbh/roadshow/appraisals*
Searchable database of the more than 6,000 past appraisals conducted by the professionals of the PBS show with a cult following

PRICE4ANTIQUES | *prices4antiques.com*
Exactly what it sounds like: a site with a full database of auction prices for antique and collectible furniture, pottery, silver, glass, clocks, lighting, paintings, prints, and more

ESTATE SALES

ESTATESALES.NET | *estatesales.net*

The best resource for finding out about upcoming estate sales in every part of the country

ESTATESALES.ORG | *estatesales.org*

Similar idea, different website (plus, you can search for items by category—jewelry, glass/crystal, rugs—rather than just location)

SHIPPING

ONLINE SHIPPING CALCULATOR | *onlineshippingcalculator.com*

A virtual calculator that allows you to compare shipping rates for packages sent via UPS, FedEx, and USPS

PIRATE SHIP | *pirateship.com*

Web-based platform that lets users buy labels for everything from letters to larger packages—usually at a fraction of the cost

USHIP | *uship.com*

Kind of like Uber, but for shipping large items (art, pieces of furniture, etc.). You can post an item you need shipped and where it's headed, and you'll be matched with someone who can pick it up and deliver it (generally for a much lower cost than a larger, white-glove shipping service)

DESIGN INSPO

The following are a few of my favorite sources for inspo, whether I'm trying to get an idea for what's trending or look at how other people in the world are styling their own homes.

→ Apartment Therapy
→ *Architectural Digest*
→ *Domino*
→ EyeSwoon
→ Houzz
→ *Lonny*
→ Pinterest
→ Style by Emily Henderson

Acknowledgments

Agnes, you are the best: a great friend, with a terrific eye for design and such a wide range of skills. I am so happy to have you as a friend and to have your support and talent on this project.

Tommy, thanks for never saying no to a spur-of-the-moment trip to the hardware store and for humoring me when I bubble over with excitement about my latest finds. You're the best picture hanger in the biz (though your curtain-hanging skills could use some work; we'll get you some training before the next book).

Gwynne, thanks for giving me the best hair (and perfecting the windblown look with just a piece of cardboard). You're the best hype man.

Kimtasha, you made me look good. Bless you for that.

Lindsay, how thrilling to work on this project with someone who is so talented, communicative, and interested in the big wide world of vintage. I'm so happy I got to meet you and work with you.

Megan, you are so talented. Thank you for bringing this project to life with your design.

Mom, thanks for always being such a good thrifting partner and willing to help me lug pieces in and out of antiques stores. Love you.

Driftwood Market, Goodwill of Northeast Florida, and Temporium: Thank you SO MUCH for allowing us to shoot in your wonderful spaces. Long live vintage.

And to the entire team at Blue Star Press, thanks for taking a chance on me and my Big Thrift Energy.

ABOUT THE ART

I started selling my own artwork several years ago, after I had found success selling vintage art. But I also create works just for fun, to hang on my own walls if I ever happen to have empty wall space, or to gift to friends. My inspiration comes (surprise!) from older works — like those by Picasso and Matisse — but also from words and language (I am a writer, after all) and the vibrant colors of the Postmodern movement. It's also all an echo of my own personal style, which means it doesn't take itself too seriously.

Virginia's artwork can
be found at Chairish,
Artfully Walls, and
Anthropologie

A

ABOUT THE AUTHOR

Virginia Chamlee is a writer, artist, and vintage addict from northeast Florida. Her home has been featured in Apartment Therapy and Design*Sponge. Her written work has been featured in publications such as *People* and the *Washington Post* and on BuzzFeed and Eater. Her art is available via Chairish, Artfully Walls, and Anthropologie. Many of her vintage finds can be found on Chairish.

She can be found on Instagram (@vchamlee), if she's not out thrifting.